OBLIGATION
A Social Theory

Obligation

A Social Theory

by Ralph Ross

Ann Arbor
The University of Michigan Press

FOR HERBERT W. SCHNEIDER

TEACHER, COLLEAGUE, AND FRIEND

Contents

Introduction

This is a book about obligation, not freedom, but neither can be treated without the other. In one way, obligation and freedom are polar opposites: freedom is an absence of constraint, and obligation is constraining. What is obligatory is somehow binding, but it is not binding as force is binding, nor is it binding even as law is, when law is backed by force and its violation brings punishment. For superior force cannot be disobeyed, law can be, at the risk of punishment, but obligation can indeed be violated, and its violation may bring no punishment at all, not even a sleepless night. So although obligation may be opposed to freedom, as all bonds are, it is not so starkly opposed as law or force. "You ought not" is not so strong a statement as "You may not," and "You ought" is different from "You shall."

Paradoxically, obligation cannot exist without freedom. Unless one is free not to do something, he cannot be obligated to do it. "You ought" implies "You are free not to." Force can and does exist without freedom, for it eliminates freedom. The law does too, when it can; armed robbery is stopped by the police, when possible. One is not merely punished for breaking a law, but violently suppressed if caught at it.

To act under obligation is to act freely. Response to obligation is the measure of a man, and requires self-restraint and self-discipline, in some cases anguish. Yet the conditions for obligation are not just the absence of external restraint and perhaps the presence of external discipline, but also the absence of internal necessity. For if everything we do is what, psychologically, we must do, there is no freedom not to do it; and "You ought" loses all meaning if it is false that "You are free not to."

So we must deal, and should deal first, with the internal or psychic conditions for obligation. I grant that a great moral philosopher, Spinoza, as well as others of considerable stature, believed in psychic necessity, the determinism of human behavior, and still believed in ethics, but that is an ethics I cannot accept. It is an ethics based on a kind of "freedom" which some men attain in varying degrees, a "freedom" which amounts to acting out the necessities imposed externally, as would be the case if all human action were necessary responses to external stimuli. What I object to is what follows (although not with logical necessity), that self-determined men must seek their own interests, however intelligently, and are limited only by power, not obligation, for there is no genuine obligation in Spinoza, not even an obligation to keep a promise made voluntarily. Instead of the great amoral morality of Spinoza, all social life seems to me based on genuine morality, whose core is obligation, and whose condition for existence is choice, and so freedom to choose.

There is another thesis about morality and determinism, found in philosophers like Dewey, which I can accept in part. The thesis is that morality cannot exist in a completely undetermined world, because no action would be more likely to attain an end than any other action, and fulfillment of obligation would be only a ritual gesture. I quarrel chiefly with "undetermined world." Change "undetermined" to "unpredictable" and matters improve greatly. There are at least two reasons for this. First, predictability is the issue in choosing means to ends; if I cannot predict that A will yield B, and B is the end I desire, there is no reason to choose A. The fact of prediction does not guarantee determinism. We predict about classes or aggregates of events, and we predict with probability, not certainty. No matter how great the probability that the Seventh Ward will vote Republican in the coming election, we cannot tell from that alone how Fotheringay, who lives in the Seventh Ward, will vote.

Second, even if all events external to human behavior were absolutely determined, it does not follow that we understand that determination enough to make any predictions. Yet human action, to be initiated in order to attain ends, depends not just on the existence of a causal sequence, let alone determinism, but on knowledge of that sequence, on predictability.

So I find it necessary to try to show the follies and limits of determinism, and of the masked determinism in much psychological behaviorism and sociological behavioralism. That is in the body of the book. In this introduction I might suggest that even people who deny determinism often assume it in one part of their minds. America and England, perhaps, cling most tenaciously to the doctrine and there may be a reason for it that should be suggested here, for it would be out of place later in dealing with determinism more formally. Tocqueville saw the effects of democracy on philosophy, religion, art, and science. Is there perhaps an effect on the treatment of causation, he asked, and, consequently, on the writing of history? In autocratic societies it is easy to find one or more men responsible for important decisions. On the battlefield, Napoleon gave orders for his cavalry to charge the enemy's flank; and the Sun King, with or without advice, made political decisions that affected Europe.

In democratic societies, the power of any individual over the social order seems much slighter. So we are more likely to explain events as the results of social forces, i.e., as external to individual decision. For those with little sense of history, what exists in their own society seems natural; it might also seem natural that human events occur without human decision or responsibility, so helpless are we all, in democracies, to determine events. The scientist, physical and social, is notoriously ahistorical in his thinking anyway (Ernst Cassirer said "There is in the Cartesian mind a kind of natural distrust, almost an antipathy, for history"), and is tempted to see the conditions of his time, or the human being of his time whom he studies, as typical of a universal order. An obvious example is the first Kinsey Report, which dealt only with twentieth-century Americans, yet was published under the title, *Sexual Behavior in the Human Male.*

More important than the influence of democracy on the idea of social causation is the image of science. To create social science that conforms to the prevailing image of science is to treat all human behavior as instances of general laws. The presupposition, almost obviously, is that all human behavior is determined, that it must be what it is. The implicit argument is not that human behavior has been examined and shown to be deterministic, nor that the thesis of determinism has been proved; it is that a behavioral science à la Newton must be possible (why? because we want it so much?) and therefore human behavior must be determined. The image of a more or less Newtonian science of man has haunted thinkers from the seventeenth century on. Later, the great successes of Smith and Ricardo in economics seemed to show that behavioral science conceived in imitation of natural science was indeed possible; this despite the fact that economics was not a behavioral science. David Hume, Smith's friend and mentor, wrote an essay with a revealing title, "That Politics Can Be Reduced to a Science." Reduced? Did all behavior have to be "reduced" to become science? Hume and Hartley reduced psychology to a science on the basis of the laws of association. Jeremy Bentham reduced morality to a science on the basis of the principle of utility. John Stuart Mill argued in his *Logic* not only that we could have a moral science but that it was by nature deductive, thus belying his own practice.

Again, sociology, politics, psychology, in order to be sciences à la Newton, had to predict human behavior with accuracy by the application of general laws. And how can that be done unless behavior is rigidly determined? How can it be done unless teleology, values, and duties are expunged, except insofar as values and duties at least are treated only externally, in objective study? As for morality, it could be a science only on the same assumptions. The special problem about moral science, which no one would face for years, is that if it must assume human determinism, its subject could not be morality, which depends on choice. In our own day, many people understand that there is either a moral science like all other sciences or else morality is based on choice, which assumes some freedom, and in that case there can be no moral science. As it became very clear that the latter is true the idea of a possible moral science was given up.

This might seem a happy ending to a somewhat idiotic tale. One might expect intelligent people to grant the possibility of moral knowledge while denying the possibility of an exact moral science, deductive or inductive. And surely there must be such people. But many social scientists and philosophers of science managed a ludicrous conclusion from the rejection of a science of morals. Their emotional investment in the mystique of exact science brought the assumption that man either has a science of something or no knowledge of it at all; it followed that the impossibility of moral science proved the impossibility of any moral knowledge, and in the absence of any moral knowledge there could be no morality, for without knowledge there is no reason whatever to make one choice rather than another. Folkways and mores, yes, for there are sciences called anthropology and sociology, but morals, no.

Finally, in order to make a set of social sciences which would be like Newtonian-style natural science, the materials studied (people, and their actions) would have to be alike in almost all ways. All experiments should, ideally, be repeatable (replicable is the current word) and come out in the same fashion always; after all, chemical elements always combine in the same way under the same conditions, and similar things should be true about men. Even if all men do not do the same things in the same circumstances, there are classes, groups, and types of men who do. Different types of chemical elements react differently, too. Scientific intelligibility required sameness, so there must be sameness. Who would question the possibility of scientific intelligibility? David Hume, in his role as historian, argued that one must assume that human motivation was always approximately the same or else a historian could not understand why people in a remote past acted as they did. Hume himself was assuming that historiography was possible and that it bore the Newtonian stamp, as far as it could. Without the Newtonian stamp we might try to discover the beliefs and values of another age in such a way that imagination and sympathy might propose and understand motivations unlike ours.

There is a great distance between the feeling of external causation in democratic societies where responsibility is hard to establish and people seemed determined by such things as social forces and the assumption underlying Newtonian social science that men are almost as alike as grains of sand. The former does lead to some contradiction of the democratic ethos—what, for example, does it mean to vote if everyone's vote is externally determined?—but the democratic core is fairly well retained. The latter moves in the direction of government by public opinion poll, and the results of each poll should be predictable in advance by the social scientist who studies the conditions of the moment.

If the aim of the elected politician is, fundamentally, to remain in office, he does what the polls demand. This is not democracy, but government by convulsive twitch.

Lord Lindsay, who also thought that one kind of social science required the assumption of human similarity and that assumption was potentially anti-democratic, put the assumption concisely ". . . the scientist, when he approaches social questions is always apt to regard human nature other than his own as being atomistic and homogeneous. The more it is so the more it is ready for the impress of his experimenting genius."

The problems of moral theory today are in great part a result of the conviction that moral statements cannot be based on facts, that "ought" cannot be derived from "is." Later I shall examine this conviction, too, more formally. In the meantime I want to comment that this is in part a result of our image of science, which has no moral "ought," but that an added inducement to believe it comes from our religious heritage, in which "ought" is not derived from the condition of man and never changes as the facts of that condition change, but has a supernatural source, and is to be accepted whatever its actual consequences on earth. When the supernatural source is denied or forgotten, the distinction between its "ought" and the world's "is" too often remains absolute. The Hobbesian moral revolution, so stoutly attacked by all good people for so long, rested on the shocking attempt to base obligation on the condition of man and the nature of society.

Here a parenthetical confession may be in order: I am stating all this in extreme terms, yet they describe the basic intellectual positions from which people move toward what they actually say and do. When they refuse to recognize the positions as their own, it is sometimes because they lack intellectual rigor, and sometimes because they realize difficulties in the basic positions, which they forget later. My extreme terms may be thought of as "models" of belief, ideas articulated without the qualifications made in actual cases. I do not think such "models" are always helpful, but in the world of ideas they do show the full logical statement underlying diluted or modified versions of a belief. So I shall continue with my "extreme" statement.

There are psychic rewards for accepting determinism and

denying the possibility of moral theory, which are received happily by people who may otherwise judge all political behavior morally, and demand of kindred souls the will to change society. What does the determinist get from his belief? Either a denial of his own responsibility and so an escape from morality, or a chance to play God, to manipulate others to become as he wants them. And both are possible: the manipulator has no one and no idea to be responsible to in his manipulations. The one who is manipulated need not mind: his genes and his environment manipulate him anyway. Why not be manipulated by a person or persons, who are only part of the environment?

The logical consequences of this situation in terms of morality are frightful. Every tin-pot Hitler, every robber baron, is exonerated for his conduct. That does not mean one should not shoot them; only that in doing so one has no moral excuse, yet is equally exonerated. Conduct then becomes a matter of power and opportunity. The wells of motivation, we are told, overflow in reward and are dammed in punishment (the hedonist's pleasure and pain decked out in the words of a new psychology). Where does the idea of God come from? Fear of punishment, elaborately manipulated? The love of music? Desire for a reward to which the subject is conditioned?

But truth matters above all, we are told, no matter how disagreeable the draught, and this simplification of behavior and history is seen as truth. Why did William invade England? For the same reason a child will do much for a candy bar. Empires and candy bars must be capable of the same treatment, for science seeks general explanations and cannot allow particular exceptions.

Second, for what real conduct is still like: what happens when statesmen and businessmen look to science, or to much contemporary philosophy to help guide their conduct? What happens to future statesmen and businessmen who are being trained in college and university now? They are either justified in almost anything they want to do or, much more likely, live in an unreliable tension between what "science" seems to imply and the conventional morality of the church, home, and social custom. Since the ingrained habits of customary morality win out in most cases, and become mere words to justify conduct not based on them in others, there is nothing in society except occasional personal re-

flection to purge and clarify morality, to adapt it to changed
conditions, and to state new and more viable principles. There is,
in brief, little genuine moral theory that is usable.

Must moral theory be usable? No; it can be an end product
of reflection, to be contemplated like a tapestry or a sunset.
Should moral theory be usable? Yes; no other intellectual matter
in our time is more important. We have used up most of the
intellectual capital of religious and traditional moralities. The interest was spent long ago. We must replenish our capital and show
how it can be used, and I attempt in this book to do some of
both. In writing a moral theory I may be writing chiefly for philosophers; in writing of social use for social scientists; I hope both
parts speak to the educated layman, who carries our hopes and
probably exists.

So far I have written about moral philosophy. But there are
some things I want to say, by way of introduction, about social
use and conduct, too. Two great limits on men in our time are (1)
the limit on the breadth of knowledge, on vision, on large views,
which limit I call specialization; and (2) the limit on control of
our destinies, on the power of men collectively, on concern for
the consequences of action, which I call drift. The two go together, of course: specialization takes away the chance to stop drift,
for that would require breadth and the large view; drift increases
the chances of growing specialization, for it offers little scope for
anything more.

Specialization is the intellectual equivalent of the economic
division of labor, and has proved just as fertile, producing far more
than could be turned out by men who did everything for themselves, and making the polymath as rare as a Swiss Family
Robinson in the suburbs. As a systematic way of ordering our
intellectual lives, specialization had its origin in the nineteenth
century and its great development in the twentieth. No longer is a
scholar, like the *philosophes* of the Enlightenment, expected to
write philosophy, economics, drama, verse, history, and fiction,
and perhaps compose operas as well; he is expected to use all his
mental energy on a single aspect of knowledge, to form his powers
into a laser beam of the mind. The result has been the knowledge
explosion, with its attendant technology, and the consequent increase in the speed of social change.

Specialization, too, is accelerating as its results are more in demand, and as rewards for the specialist grow greater, and this will, in turn, speed up the rate of social change still more. Our strange, wonderful, perhaps unique situation is shot through with paradox. The better we do, the worse things are. As a result of the motor car, more of us bleed on the highway than in war and most of us strangle in the city, which is rapidly becoming uninhabitable. As a result of medical science, the planet itself may soon be uninhabitable. The problem is mortality, not food production. If we could produce enough food for the billions of people who will be on earth in a few years, they would have to stand on each other's shoulders.

So we come to the question of directing our activities, a matter of much confusion. We are misled, perhaps, by an analogy to the great success of a free economy, in which we make whatever we can make and sell whatever we can sell, with little thought of consequence. Just so, we accept all conveniences and comforts in the happy thought that whatever their cost in life or in natural resources—how much longer will our oil supplies last?—Science will provide. The more specialized we are, the less capable we become of understanding the relations and movements, the total configuration of our society. Yet without some grasp of the whole, we are poorly placed to suggest directions and controls. Unfortunately, humility is not always bred by success, and the famous physicist speaks about politics, as the psychologist speaks about art, with all the assurance of a motion-picture actress explaining the values of civilization—and too often, about as well.

We cannot give up specialization, and its incalculable fruits, but we must counterbalance it so we can correct its errors, chide its arrogance, and control its results. And the counterbalance should not come only from others, but from the specialist, too, who often needs it within, himself, for the specialization of knowledge is also the fragmentation of mind.

From the other side, that of drift, we paid an enormous price to have the Industrial Revolution, without knowing what it was or whether we wanted it. No one understood what was happening when the Industrial Revolution started, and the organization of society was such that little could be done had we understood. The price we paid included widespread misery, actual starvation, brutality, and the destruction of community. When the Industrial Revolution presumably occurred, it moved almost too slowly to be a revolution, but it gathered momentum and became a continuous revolution; the result is that we are still paying somewhat for its very existence. What was paid in the beginning of the nineteenth century is only intimated by the three official reports presented to the English Parliament in 1832 and 1842 on child labor in factories and mines; like parts of Zola's *Germinal,* they present a prose *Inferno.*

What we are paying now is the price for having had the Industrial Revolution. The price has gone up. It may include the destruction of the human race. And neither price was necessary. We drifted into the price as we drifted into the Industrial Revolution itself.

So the crisis of our times seems to me much bound up with specialization and drift. We all have difficulty riding the whirlwind, adjusting constantly to the new as the pace of change mounts. And we are fearful of the morrow because our change is undirected, and the morrow may bring almost anything. We are lonesome in the loss of an educated community, men knowing many of the same things, reading the same books, having a continuous conversation about ideas. It is quite possible today at many colleges for students to graduate with few books and fewer ideas in common. Their professors exist in almost airtight communities of specialization: the classicist is not supposed to know the bare elements of physics, and the physicist is not expected even to recognize names like Ovid and Horace.

The excitement of the specialist at work is great, and so are the rewards for intellectual discovery. But as teacher, the specialist just perpetuates his own image in the next generation. The undergraduate in the specialists' hands is taught *all* his subjects as though he were a potential graduate or professional school student—in increasing numbers he is, in *one* of his subjects—and is equipped with the primal tools of several crafts, although he may practice none of them. In the process, knowledge becomes information, or data, and thought becomes method. The mind itself, by functioning in little, windowless compartments, is trivialized. The great issues of human existence are untouched—their very existence ignored, and sometimes denied—except as tiny parts of them slip into the problems of specialists.

I have overstated the case again, but enough of the case is true so that students through the country are protesting the meaninglessness or triviality of their studies. Youth is a generous age, readily attracted by the great themes of history and the fervor of dedication. Youth needs the sobriety of intellectual discipline so the themes can be analyzed and understood, and the dedication given to what is worthy. But with no themes at all, and no objects of dedication except a specialized scientific or scholarly pursuit, youth easily grows restive and seeks what it desires elsewhere, outside the academy; or it demands power to make changes within the academy, though, in the nature of youth, it has little notion what the changes should be.

I take the unrest of our time seriously. I do not think it is just another generational revolt or a temporary disenchantment with our political leaders. It is a genuine malaise, resulting from intellectual bankruptcy in our moral, political, and philosophical outlooks. It is not the academy alone that is bankrupt, but the mind of our day. I will be dealing with intellectual issues that arise in the academy because I think it important to show what is wrong with many of our ingrained ideas, and also because this is the first society of mass education, and the academy, which now has the power, does little to cure the malaise, indeed contributes to it.

To detail the negative contributions of the academy would require another book. Let me mention two, the first of which has to do with language. Language has become a basic subject for many philosophers, linguistics has become a study of its own, with ramifications like psycholinguistics, and some behavioral scientists rely heavily on questionnaires. There is, to the discerning eye and ear, great wealth in the nuances of language. What a man says, however hastily, bears marks of a meaning not explicitly stated, perhaps not even intended. The academy, in its official and unofficial guises, has devised true and false examinations and multiple choice examinations which require no linguistic answers, only check marks. And what of I.Q. tests, public opinion polls, and questionnaires? More check marks, not language, despite the intimate connection between the development of self and the development of one's use of language. Aristotle thought that a talent for metaphor was a sign of genius, for it showed a sense of connections in the world. But there can be no metaphor if we do not speak or write, and a written check mark is the equivalent of a verbal grunt.

There is much more to be said about this, but I will summarize only a few things. The choice of question demanding a grunt or check mark in response often brings an answer in which one doesn't believe, because the options were too few. Also, one answers questions which he never asked himself, and which therefore have no real significance to him. The student, or respondent, is stunted in the growth normally brought by thought and language, and stunted in finding significance, which depends on the questions he asks himself.

As for the second academic "contribution" that should at least be mentioned: perhaps nothing we teach is more harmful than our reduced image of ourselves—taught implicitly, perhaps, more than explicitly—which makes reflection unimportant and action insignificant, and provokes a response that is thoughtless but fervent. Basic to this reduction of man is the amputation of his moral dimension—in the large sense, not just that of price-fixing, judicial bribery, or premarital sex. Questions of ends, ideals, goals, justice, order and liberty, obligation and advantage, elude us, but they are our great questions. What we have done to evade them is to deny either their significance or our powers.

In order to treat these questions, I have written the first two chapters as preliminaries to the inquiry. The principle of limited categories, with which I start, is a device that makes clear what the specialist can and cannot do. It also permits me to deal with the problems that overflow scientific disciplines as they are now understood by using all categories and terms that are relevant. The narrowness of focus in particular social sciences is a hallmark of the academic mind of our day, a one-eyed vision being protested— if I read the signs correctly—most often implicitly, by many bright, younger scholars who chafe at unnecessary restraints in pursuing their ideas.

The rest of the book is far from exhaustive; its argument is sufficient, I hope, to be the base of a program to be continued by many minds in many ways, some of which I try to indicate. Those who cannot accept any of it are probably satisfied with the current state of philosophy and social science, as I am not, or find those studies irrelevant to the struggles of men, except perhaps as explanatory.

As for the style: some few parts of my subject require a technical analysis, and so are written somewhat technically; other parts do not require such analysis and are not written technically. That makes for a book uneven in difficulty and rigor. But if one writes of many things, he may be consoled by remembering Aristotle's dictum that "it is the mark of an educated man to look for precision in each class of things just so far as the nature of the subject admits." I have not tried to impose an artificial unity of style but have tried to write of each class of things as the nature of the subject admits.

CHAPTER ONE

The Principle of Limited Categories

The importance of the belief in psychic determinism for the very possibility of morality should be clear enough by now to show that examination of its meaning and truth are vital. A theory of obligation, which comes later, can be stated with less qualification if other matters, such as a close look at determinism, come first. I should like to come at those other matters somewhat indirectly, for the sake of effectiveness.

Arguments against psychic determinism should gain in power and persuasiveness if there is a principle about science to appeal to. Such a principle can be constructed by attending to the basic concepts of each of the sciences, natural and social. These concepts enter language as terms, i.e., words or phrases, which may identify the science that uses them regularly: e.g., "gravitation" is important to physics and astronomy, but means nothing, except perhaps metaphorically, in economics. The terms in which a science is carried on are basic, derivative, or loosely related to each other. Basic terms are those to which many of the others are reducible or under which they can be classified; they are fundamental to explanation in a science; they may be called categories.

Physics was once defined (who would dare define it in any way now?) as the science of matter and motion, so light and sound, both of which were studied in physics, were presumably thought to be classifiable under matter and motion. Matter and motion, then, were categories of physics. They also marked out and limited a subject matter. It is the matter in a living organism that can be studied in physics, not its animate qualities, which are studied in biology and psychology.

If one could make a neat list of the categories of any science, he would have an implicit definition of its subject, for a subject is what can be studied profitably by the use of a given set of categories. In one sense, the same subject can be studied by use of different sets of categories: living organisms can be studied in terms of physics, chemistry, zoology, physiology, psychology, and in some cases, sociology. In another sense, each of these sciences has, by virtue of its categories, a different subject matter. There is no problem about the two senses of subject matter I have used. The first sense is the large one in which each subject is composed of wholes, or entities, like organisms, people, societies. The second sense is one in which aspects of these comprise a subject, like chemical action and reaction, or the production and distribution of wealth. The category set in each science is limited in number, and if there is any overlap of categories with another science, it is minor. Clearly, the conclusions of each science should be limited to that aspect of a whole or large subject to which its categories apply, and should not be applied to the subject as a whole, for which other category sets are also needed. This I call the principle of limited categories. We shall see how casually social scientists apply what they learn about one aspect of human behavior to the large subject, man, a subject matter in my first sense. In a simple, nonsocial instance, astronomy and astrology deal with the same large subject matter (in different ways and with different aspects); astronomy properly avoids predictions of human destiny (unless it were to predict such a thing as the destruction of the earth) and astrology should not include speculation about nebular distances.

Whatever its value in natural science, the principle of limited categories is useful in social and humanistic matters, where the same subject is constantly studied under different categories, and so by different conceptual schemes. Electrons and chromosomes are not so readily treated under the categories of morals or politics as they are under the categories of physics and genetics, but the decisions of a business corporation may be, and are, studied by conceptual schemes based on moral and political categories as well as by conceptual schemes based on economic categories. A painting may be studied in the terms of aesthetics, art history, business, sociology, or history; it can be treated as art, investment, or document. But if we use aesthetic categories, and decide that a

painting is a great masterpiece, it is then illegitimate on the basis
of that decision alone—adding no other categories—to conclude
that the painting was enormously influential in shaping artistic
style, or that it reveals a great deal about the age in which it was
created. In the same way, a business decision that is excellent in
purely economic terms may be morally repulsive and politically
dangerous, and it may be all three at once.

Just as astronomers would deny the relevance or usefulness
of applying astrological categories to their subject matter, so social
scientists might deny the relevance or usefulness of applying non-
scientific categories to their subject matter. What of ethics, law, or
religion, for example, none of which is normally called a science?
Is it not as important for social science to be rid of their categories as it once was for natural science to be rid of the category
of teleology? As stated, that is a muddled issue. Social scientists
need use no categories but their own in their science; they can be
rid of any categories they come to regard as unscientific. The real
question is that of the *legitimacy* of other (extrascientific) studies
of men and society, those, for example, which use the categories
assumed by ethics, by law, or by religion. To deny their legitimacy
is to extend the application of the conclusions of social science
to man *per se* and society *per se*, however we conceive them,
instead of limiting the conclusions to an aspect of man and society
implicitly defined by the categories of social science. When the
conclusions are extended in their application, there is implicit
denial of any aspects of man and society other than those studied
by social science, for otherwise there would be different conclusions, and by that denial the latter cease to be aspects of man and
society and become the entire subject. In effect, man and society
are thus redefined. This extension of the subject matter of social
science, still more extreme in individual social sciences, implies
that its categories are the only, or *the* correct categories for
dealing with man and society; it is a violation of the principle of
limited categories, since other sets of categories are relevant to the
subject matter, and can help us answer questions about it that fall
outside social science.

In some ways, social scientists who deny the validity of
moral categories are more candid and courageous than philosophers who also deny them, for the social scientists then admit

they do not believe in the existence of morals, while few of the philosophers make the same admission (although logically they must). The social scientists often go on to suggest alternatives to morals, like scientific control of man (to what ends only God knows), while philosophers (e.g., logical positivists) restate the meaning of moral propositions in nonmoral terms, as when they translate "you ought to" into "I would prefer you to." Thus they eliminate all moral quality, or move from ethics to an analysis of the meaning of ethical terms, asking such things as the different ways in which we use the word "punishment" (e.g., ordinary language philosophers), or concern themselves only with meta-ethics, whose subject is ideas or systems of ethics, not human conduct and value. Although this situation is pervasive, its meaning is neglected; it deserves close attention, for its consequences in life might be drastic, but only if people took social science and philosophy seriously. That few people do is a comment on the power and sophistication of contemporary social science and philosophy in dealing with morals.

To some contemporaries, the denial of choice and responsibility, and so of morals, does not seem at all outrageous, but rather the hard-headedness and candor of scientists in a world misled into superstition by its history. This view of some scientists—it cannot be called a scientific view—is a genuine romanticism with more attractiveness to today's scientific intellectuals than almost all other romanticisms together. It is a denial of fact by theory, a reach that exceeds its grasp, and an attitude of false stoicism. Its charm is that it presents itself as antiromantic, even austere, dedicated to the truth, however it hurts to accept the "truth" in place of the fictions (read "facts") we love so. It is for the "tough-minded," who are so often sentimental.

A youthful natural science is invoked by the romantics of social science, who repeat its Democritean pattern and take strength from its rejection of human illusion. "How deep the green of those leaves," one murmurs in midsummer; and is answered, "Green is in fact only one wave frequency among others. What you are talking about is not really there on the leaves; it is merely your physiological response to the wave frequencies as they impinge on the senses." "And the tree, its branches, the leaves themselves?" "All that is there is molecular motion; the illusion of trees may be inescapable, but that makes it no less an illusion." Now if we can deny the existence of trees, how can we balk at the denial of morals?

We may think we have choice, says the scientific romantic, but we also think we see trees. And we can deny trees in so many ways: we can reduce them without residue to molecular motion; we can insist they are psychological constructs put together out of primitive sense-data, which are all we really experience; we can conceivably argue (some scientists have come close) that seeing trees as we do is a relative cultural trait, inextricably connected with an early belief in hamadryads. And we can deny morals in at least as many ways: we can say that since man is a creature whose actions are all caused, he has no freedom of choice, and so no responsibility, and in consequence no morals; or we can argue that the word "ought" can have no empirical meaning since it describes nothing factual, and no analytic meaning because it does not enter logical relations with "is" (that is, premises all containing "is" yield a conclusion also containing "is," and never a conclusion containing "ought," because conclusions can contain nothing that is not in the premises). Thus the meaning of "ought" can only be psychological: every time any one says "You ought to do that," what he means is "I would be pleased if you did it."

All this distinction between human folly and truth, folly being the facts before every man's eyes and truth being sheer theory, is an old metaphysic of appearance and reality (already extreme at the beginning of the fifth century B.C., when Parmenides told his shattering truth, that nothing really moved) stated in terms of current science. Surely it is not itself science, but a metaphysic of scientists. The temptation to indulge in it seems irresistible. We learn again and again, from good scientists indeed, that the great pressure of historical and social forces (reality) turns the deliberations, agreements, and treaties of statesmen (appearance) into the illusion of control. (Another blow at the importance of moral choice and human decision.) We also learn, for Hans Morgenthau tells us, that politics is determined "not by moral principles and legal commitments [appearance] but by considerations of interest and power [reality]." We are left to wonder whether historical and social forces exist apart from human action or whether "*considerations* of interest and power" are not necessarily some people's *ideas* of the national interest and the nation's relative power. Why they have these ideas, how true they are, and how it is that certain people's ideas guide national policy while other people's ideas do not, are still other problems, as is the larger and fascinating question of the power of ideas, which seems neglected, to say the least. But "considerations" at least sneaks human decisions back into the social pattern, even though it is not moral decision.

Another way to dispense with morals is indirect; it is an utterly contemporary (which may mean momentary) argument made by many philosophers. To quote one of them: "A . . . line of attack that has forced ethicists to avoid normative theorizing . . . is the contention that all attempts to develop theories of moral obligation are foredoomed to failure, because it is logically impossible to give reasons in support of our convictions about what we ought to do."* The point, of course, is that reasons for what we *ought* to do are devoid of *oughts* themselves and are full of *is's*. As H. A. Prichard wrote in 1912, in a now-renowned essay, "Does Moral Philosophy Rest on a Mistake": "An 'ought' . . . can only be derived from another 'ought'." It does not take much acumen to see that if *theories* of moral obligation will not wash because we cannot logically give reasons for what we ought to do, and so no *particular* moral obligation can be supported with reasons, then there are no moral obligations at all, only such things as conventions and commands, to guide conduct. It must follow there can be no morality. Logically, a moral situation involves choice, and choice requires reasons, not just greater socialization to one convention or command than to another.

One may quite legitimately reject all theories that dispense with morals, explicitly or implicitly, by appeal to the facts. They show that life is drenched in morality, and there is no legitimate escape from moral problems. The place of morality in life and society requires explanation, to be sure, but it is not an explanation of morality to deny it, even though we argue that the conditions for its existence—choice, for example, or the possibility of

---

*Journal of the History of Philosophy, Vol. V, No. 1, January, 1967, p. 107. I think it unimportant to mention the author's name; besides, he may learn better.

offering reasons for making one rather than another moral decision—do not themselves exist. For that is like interrupting a
discussion of the power of nationalism with the comment that
such power is illusory because there are no nations. Nations, after
all, are alleged to have a common history, language, ethnic stock,
and geographical limits. If it can be shown that the history of
Massachusetts is in part English history, while that of California is
in part Spanish, that local speech differences are tantamount to
different languages, that European, Asian, and African ethnic
stocks are all to be found in America, and that the borders of the
United States are open to question (e.g., by the Iroquois), can it
then be maintained successfully that the United States is not a
nation, and for similar reasons that there are no other nations?
And then, of course, that there are no national wars? It cannot; all
that can be established is that the conditions for nationhood or
the ingredients in the definition of a nation need further study.

To deny morality, or to deny nations, is to start an intellectual enterprise in the wrong place. If a group of conditions for the
existence of anything, say X, are the result of general agreement,
and are then challenged with some effectiveness, one cannot reasonably argue that since the conditions generally recognized for
the existence of X do not obtain, X does not exist, although X is
in front of everyone's nose. A simpler illustration than morals or
nations is fire. If we encounter a fire under laboratory conditions
that presumably exclude oxygen, our first thought should be that
by some mistake oxygen did enter. But if many checks and repeti-
tions showed no oxygen at all, we would be faced with the
startling problem of accounting for fire, or a special form of fire,
without oxygen as a necessary condition. We would never be entitled to deny the existence of the fire we experienced, if it was
an experience open to all qualified observers.

The starting place is in experience. Fires, nations, marriages,
wars, morals demand explanation. Many explanations have been
offered, and at any given time some one explanation is likely to
have general acceptance. If that explanation is then challenged, the
burden of proof rests on the challenger. Can he really establish his
case? If he can, the next step is to offer a new explanation, in
terms of other conditions for the occurrence or existence of the
phenomenon. If that is unsuccessful, we might ask whether what

we are talking about is perhaps not a typical instance of the phenomenon, but a special case. We are still not entitled to start
backwards, with the conditions or the explanation, rather than the
phenomenon to be explained, and by denying the conditions generally accepted at the time, deny the existence of the phenomenon
itself. But just this is done by those who deny the existence of
morals, for they deny such conditions of morality as free choice,
and then conclude that the phenomenon, morality, cannot exist.

Still another way of rejecting the dismissal of important
areas of life, like morality, is a test to discover whether the principle of limited categories has been violated, whether there has been
over-generalization from a category set. If there has (if conclusions
reached within a conceptual scheme based on a limited set of
categories have been generalized to apply to the subject matter *per
se,* that is, the subject matter in its entirety and not just the
aspects of it relevant to the categories), it will be impossible to
state any conceivable conditions under which the conclusions
would be false.

A familiar instance of such a fallacy—one that is typical of
more contemporary argument—is the theory of human motivation
found in hedonist psychology. The theory is that men by their
very nature seek pleasure and try to avoid pain; all human action
is explicable in those terms; all other explanations are erroneous.
Thus love, altruism, power, ideology, and such categories are beside
the point; pleasure and pain are the only relevant terms. Human
acts that were explained under other categories have to be reex-
plained, for the other categories are branded as irrelevant. And
human nature is thus redefined.

How well does the hedonist explanation work? Examples
make that abundantly clear. If a man gives up his own advantage
to do what he thinks obligatory, that only shows—it is argued—
that the pleasure of fulfilling what he regards as his obligation is
greater than that of serving his advantage or, alternatively, that the
pain to him of not fulfilling what he thinks obligatory would
outweigh the pleasure derived from his advantage. In the extreme
case, if a man sacrifices his life for others, the explanation is that
his conscience would so pain him had he done otherwise that he
would rather die than suffer so much pain. One may conclude that
the hedonist position, when its categories are applied beyond their

relevance, can allow no conceivable conditions under which it could be proved false and that, in consequence, it cannot legitimately prove its case. No theory is acceptable, after all, if no *conceivable* event could falsify it, although if it is true no *actual* event will falsify it. Power-theorists, of the sort Nietzsche sometimes is, are logically in the same case as hedonists.

For the hedonist, or the power-theorist, to extricate himself from the trap just described, it is only necessary that he observe the principle of limited categories. He may, instead, prefer to over-generalize and to state what could, conceivably, invalidate it, some human act which, if it occurred, would constitute refutation of his theory. But if the act is possible to man, man has actually done it, and the theory will be promptly refuted. If, however, the hedonist limits his generalization to man insofar as he actually seeks pleasure and tries to avoid pain—in economics, in sex, in games,—in short, insofar as he talks only of hedonistic man, an important aspect of the human being, he may tell us much of consequence. When profit, in all its senses, is identified with pleasure, economic man is one kind of hedonistic man, and much has been learned by assuming that economic man has a tendency to improve his material conditions.

Among some contemporary social scientists (and some humanists, too, needless to say) limited categories are employed to yield too-general conclusions. One extremely important instance is the use of behaviorist psychology and some types of sociology to reinstate the philosophy of determinism. As a scientific dream, determinism is probably unobjectionable; like other dreams, it motivates work which may turn out good and, in the end, it still must be tested against reality. But when it is argued that determinism is true doctrine and that its truth denies the possibility of morals as we have known it—morals based on choice and responsibility—it is more than an academic responsibility to reveal its pretensions and fallacies.

In fact, our knowledge of human behavior is such that we can sometimes explain with some probability the causes of particular actions, and can even propose hypotheses of some value about some *types* of action. It is a goal of scientific psychology—and of social science itself—to be able to explain all types of human action by discovering their causes. This goal is first converted by determinists into a statement that what they seek must exist in all cases: every human act is caused. It is then assumed that an act that is caused cannot at the same time be free, because a free act is thought to be an uncaused act, whatever that may be. If a human act, the argument continues, is caused, then it *must* be what it is; it cannot be otherwise. And that is determinism, a doctrine that we do what we must, and can do nothing else. If an objector points out that he has just done as he wishes, it is answered that that is quite possible, for he might wish what he does, but that he cannot then wish as he wishes. If I order steak from the restaurant menu, and insist that I ordered what I wanted from a large variety, the determinist's answer is that indeed steak may be what I wanted, but at that moment under those conditions, I couldn't have wanted anthing else.

This argument violates the principle of limited categories because psychology, or sociology, or any other behavioral or social science, dealing necessarily with only one aspect of man or society, is not entitled to make pronouncements about man *per se* under any and all circumstances. Then, if I am right, there should be no conceivable conditions under which its adherents would regard determinism as false, and indeed there are none. The case is the same as this: if I say, "It is raining," and there is a torrent falling from above, what I say is true, but it is at least conceivable (though false) that it is a dry, sunny day. If I then insist that that, too, like any conceivable weather condition would be proof that it is raining, I have made my original comment, "It is raining," scientifically meaningless, since a downpour no more proves its truth than dryness and sunshine would. Failure to find conditions under which my comment could be false is also failure to find conditions which prove it true. A proposition that is true under any conditions whatever is a logically necessary proposition like "Either it is raining or it is not," but it is not a factual proposition, whose truth depends on conditions being of one kind, not another.

If determinism is logically necessary, the argument for it would have to be logical or metaphysical. There have been such arguments; I do not think they are successful; and contemporary social scientists would regard themselves as traitors to science if they accepted them. The issue, we must remember, is psychic, not natural, determinism. After all, if physical nature is determined and man is not, there can be no deterministic objection to morality. So the issue must be met in psychology and the social sciences. And it has not been pursued through all the social sciences in the same way. Some psychologists, sociologists, anthropologists, and cyberneticists hold the doctrine, but historians for the most part do not sing the praises of historical inevitability, which is determinism in history. Those in social science and philosophy who do cling to determinism accept no possible refutation of the doctrine, however imaginary, and so can show nothing that proves it.

Point to an act that *seems* uncaused and one is told promptly that we have not yet discovered the cause, but of course we will—thus adding a *petitio principii* to the original difficulty. To apply the principle of limited categories is to shrink the application of the determinist hypothesis to those who act under inner compulsion, those who really cannot do other than they do. And then "determinism" may be of the utmost value in helping us understand actions which are of great significance in the psychic economy of some people and of some significance, perhaps, in the psychic economy of all people, because we may all be compulsive about one thing or another.

This violation of the principle of limited categories is perhaps more widespread than my argument about social science reveals. The situation for which I devised that principle bothered no less a scientist and philosopher than Alfred North Whitehead, who wrote: "Science has always suffered from the vice of overstatement. In this way, conclusions true within strict limitations have been generalized dogmatically into a fallacious universality."*

As the determinist thesis stands, it has substituted a logical pattern of necessity for an empirical pattern of probability, and has done it, curiously, in the name of empirical science. It has also changed the idea of the relation of man and nature. An older view of the world was that physical nature was determined, but man was undetermined (at the time that defined "free"). Now the situation has been reversed: the influential contemporary determinist does not deal with physical nature, he is not at all concerned about a possible physical indeterminism based on Heisenberg's "leap of the atom," but he is concerned about man. Nature may be undetermined, but man is determined.

*The Function of Reason, Beacon Press, Fifth printing, 1967, p. 27.

This strange situation, a modern scientific attack on an old theology, can be defended only by treating (a) a free act as an uncaused act and (b) a caused act as a determined act. But neither, I think, is true, unless an act based on reasons, not physical causes, is called uncaused. Then (a) is true. As for (b), suppose we define causation and determinism thus: (1) there is causation when E does occur under conditions C; (2) there is determinism when E *must* occur under conditions C. It might be argued that these are different propositions, and that (2) requires more and different evidence than (1). But that is not what the determinist claims. He asserts (a) an identity of the two propositions or (b) a necessary inference of the second from the first. Now, "does" and "must" have different meanings, and it is difficult to see how it is one and the same thing to say that something happened and that it had to happen. As for (b), some additional proposition or propositions would have to be added to make the inference legitimate. One could do so by assuming a third proposition, that all caused events *must* occur exactly as they *do* occur. But this begs the question because it is the assumption of determinism, not its proof. The determinist argument provides, in form, a close analogy to the hedonist argument and suffers from identical weaknesses, for the hedonist assumes that men *must* seek pleasure and avoid pain, not merely that in fact all men do.

We may conclude that determinism is not a scientific theory at all but a metaphysic, which is often propounded by scientists and scientific buffs. I think that what I have said refutes it, but I want to do something more. It is revealing of a whole and remarkably influential world-view to pursue the argument further, to discover some consequences of believing it, and to examine other definitions of determinism. I shall do so, starting with a negative statement of determinism: under conditions C, a man cannot do anything but E.

If the same statement were made about inanimate objects, or perhaps much simpler forms of life, the qualities of mind would not be at issue: knowledge, reason, memory, imagination, insight, etc. But in dealing with man, the determinist must maintain that mind is determined, too, in all its qualities. So a man *may* do as he wants, but he *must* want what he wants and, in that sense, both what he wants and what he does are determined. Suppose we deal in a nondeterminist way with individual human behavior in terms of knowledge. To bring something about, or to avert it, we probably need knowledge. Our predictions must be true to be used successfully in voluntary action, unless we are just lucky. If it is true that whenever C occurs E will occur, and I know it and can control the occurrence of C, then if I want E, I can create C, and if I don't want E, I can insure that C does not occur. In the latter case, C would also have to be a necessary condition for E (only if C, then E), for otherwise it might also be the case that if C_1, then E (spontaneous combustion can cause fire, but so can a match). If particular social conditions will probably increase the rate of crime, we have a chance to stop that increase by changing the conditions if we can. This is an increase in freedom because it is an increase in choice and, of course, it is an increase in power.

But determinism would have it that if we changed the social conditions that bring about an increase in crime, we did it because we were so conditioned that we had to choose to decrease crime. Suppose, however, we did our best to create social conditions for crime. Then determinism would have it that we had to try to increase crime. And if, in full knowledge of the facts, we did nothing, the determinist contention would be that we had to be apathetic or paralyzed. Since we had only three choices—to institute the conditions, to oppose the conditions, or to do neither— and whatever our choice, it turned out to be necessary according to the determinist argument, this is an example of the extent to which determinism admits no possible evidence to the contrary (and so has a case that cannot itself be supported by evidence). And the increase in freedom that knowledge brings is lost because there is no freedom, so there is nothing to increase.

Next, there are obvious instances in which habituation binds us and knowledge makes us free (although there are also cases where habituation is freeing). If a man is habituated to large quantities of liquor every night and starts to have severe hangovers in the morning, he may, knowing the connection between the two, drink less or stop drinking. If he did not know the connection, he would not know how to avoid his hangovers. As it is, he is free to choose to continue to have his hangovers so he can drink too much, or not to have hangovers and to pay the price by drinking less. Countless examples of the same kind come to mind readily, but psychotherapeutic evidence testifies to another kind of example that is perhaps even more impressive. Often, knowing the cause of feelings we find unpleasant, we seem able to make that knowledge an integral part of the personality and, in consequence, rid ourselves of the unpleasant feelings. This is an instance of knowledge, deeply felt, itself becoming a cause, not just an instance of using knowledge to create or destroy causes. Here the determinist might say some men are so conditioned that they can and must act thus, while others cannot. But this seems explanation by ingenuity, not science.

It is especially difficult to persuade determinists that categories that apply to compulsive behavior do not necessarily apply to all behavior. To show at greater length what difference in behavior can occur because of knowledge, consider another instance. If eating eggs for breakfast—although I enjoy eggs—upsets my stomach, and I know it, then my choice of breakfast food may depend on my judgment about the relative merits of that enjoyment and that upset. What is determined about this, since "determined" events *must* occur? Must I have an upset stomach? Not if I don't eat eggs for breakfast, or whatever else may upset my stomach. Must I eat eggs for breakfast? Certainly not, unless I am willing to have an upset stomach. Are there people in similar circumstances who cannot forgo eggs for breakfast when they can have them (for at times they may not be able to have them)? Perhaps. And for such people, upset stomachs are determined, for eggs they must have, they cannot do otherwise. But that is not the normal, or at least healthy, human condition; in arguments about determinism that have been made before, it is like the condition of the kleptomaniac rather than the condition of the thief.

Sophistication, today, brings other definitions of determinism, without mention of "must" or "necessity." Some contemporaries mean by "determinism" the doctrine that all human behavior can be explained in physical or mechanical terms.* Even

---

*Stuart Hampshire, for instance, uses "determinism" to name ". . . the scheme that requires experimentally confirmed laws of reasonable simplicity which correlate, with sufficient precision and determinacy, ranges of specified inputs with ranges of specified outputs from the organism." *Freedom of the Individual,* Harper & Row, 1965, pp. 108f. This presupposes, like so much other talk of human inputs and outputs, that however much the input is

then, what I have urged basically against determinism still holds: it violates the principle of limited categories. Of course, I am maintaining the irreducibility of certain categories and sets of categories, and so opposing reductions which not only redefine a subject but, in crucial instances, reject all possible contrary evidence. To determinists my argument may seem prejudiced against science, as they understand it, but it strikes me as evident that they have gone beyond genuine science, which I think I am supporting, and are sadly limiting the possibilities of science by the elimination of some terms that are indispensable to knowledge. I think, too, that scientists (especially social scientists) often develop a loyalty to their own sciences which amounts to jingoism, for it is pejorative, and so is incompatible with the full acceptance of other sciences. The belief in determinism, defined as explanation of all human behavior in physical or mechanical terms, is an elimination of much possible anthropology and sociology, or a limitation of them, such that a great deal that could be learned and explained by the determinist will not be.

The most obviously neglected areas, when one deals with behavior as input-output, are those in which human creativity, especially in the arts and humanities, require explanation in social, psychological and humanistic terms. I shall come to this in the next chapter. But it does not take the "creative" act or its products to show the limitations and weaknesses of determinist or reductionist theses, or the need to combine humanist and scientific categories. Much simpler matters serve as well. If a man believes in justice, and we want to explain that, we must explain not only "believe," but "justice" as he understands it, and that is an enterprise totally apart from the question whether he must believe in justice, can be explained in physico-chemical terms, or is a mere responder to stimuli. Then there are puzzles that arise when behavioral scientists speak boldly of explaining all human action if only they have enough information. If one can explain, he should also be able to predict, or his claim to explain is invalidated. Too often people "explain" persuasively when they cannot predict at all.

---

converted into something different by the organism, there are no outputs without inputs. In decent English, this means we never act as a result of inner motivation, reflection, or self-generated ideas, but only in response to external stimuli. Thus a Skinnerian stimulus-response psychology is implicitly justified.

With enough ingenuity one can "explain" any social occurrence in terms of the Hegelian dialectic, but still cannot predict; explanation, unlike prediction, is always after the fact, and that is sufficient to nullify the claim made for the dialectic—by Marxists, for example—that it is science. In addition, when we talk of having enough information, there is a difficulty we must face, apart from the question-begging "enough," which is that information is gathered for a purpose, even so general a purpose as compiling an encyclopedia. Much information that later might seem relevant would not be gathered because there would seem to be no reason to do so.

No matter how general the prediction is, one can predict A's behavior totally only if (1) we assume A as he is at the moment, before he has one more experience that might change him in some respect, and (2) if we know every possible kind of thing that might happen to him next. Of course, if A is changed by his next experience, one must start all over, predicting anew every reaction to every kind of thing that can happen to him; and, to say the least, no one is likely ever to know every possible thing that could happen to A next, nor is there any reason for acquiring that information, which would seem adventitious before the fact. What one can do is "explain" A's behavior after the fact but that, like the Hegelian dialectic, is not quite science, for without predictions explanations cannot be tested.

It may still be argued that one could *conceivably* know so very much about A that it would be possible to predict precisely, not generally, what he would do next. But what A does next depends on what happens to him next, and so on what he responds to. Even if what I do—to leave A for a moment—is determined, i.e., is either what I must do or, more simply, is explicable physically (or mechanically or chemically), what *happens* to me may be accident, i.e., not predictable at all. And such accidents happen all day: I am caught in a thunderstorm and die of pneumonia, I meet an old friend and discover I now hate him, I fall in love. How I respond, the determinist thinks, is predictable; but what I respond to is unanticipated; so the scientist must constantly be informed, just as contingent fact, of the situations in which I will find myself. That is impossible; the mind of God may know what will in fact be, when there is no causal pattern, but the mind of man cannot. And from man's point of view, there is always contingency. Although on the determinist case itself, every path of individual human behavior may be throughly predictable, still those paths intersect continually, and the intersection of two or more paths of behavior is contingent from the standpoint of any one of them. Examples are not difficult to find.

Suppose one were to adopt the determinist's hypothesis with no reservations. If A is a young man who walks every other day at a particular time from one building on a university campus to another, since he takes classes in both, and this is the day on which he has the two classes, he *may* (not must) walk on the same path at the same time as he did two days ago. He may not, of course, for he might have eaten eggs for breakfast and have an upset stomach, and so stay home; he may miss his classes because today he is tired of them or has decided it is more important to read or write something; he may take another path, more roundabout, because he has someone boring to avoid, or someone interesting to talk to, and his companion is going elsewhere. But assume he walks the regular path at the regular time. Add a man, B, who for reasons a psychiatrist might understand, climbs the high tower on that campus with a determination to shoot everyone in sight, and carries enough armament to do so. The result is that B shoots and kills A, along with many others. Such things could happen, since they did happen, on an American university campus. Is it really possible—apart from wild imaginings—that any scientist could ever predict A's death (death may not be behavior, but dying is, and a young man's dying thus, with nothing to indicate it in his past, leaves his dying unpredictable), even on the basis of complete information about A, which no scientist, I venture, could ever have? God could predict it, so in wild defiance of Occam's razor we have to postulate a completely known universe and an omniscient mind, if A's death is to be called determined. But could such an event be called determined in man's universe: could it conceivably be known, since there was no reason whatever to link B's action to A's? If it could not be known, it is strange to think of it as determined. To be honest, one can only call it accident in man's world, and accident is not a word that fits the determinist thesis, whether it is couched in terms of "must," of physics and chemistry, or of "input" and "output."

Knowledge, though, provides the final limitation of determinism, and knowledge, so far as I know, has not been explored as an instance of the determinist thesis so fully as action, perhaps because the results may be even more embarrassing to the determinist. It is one thing to say of the prisoner in the dock that he was so conditioned he had to commit the crime, he could not do otherwise. It is quite another thing to say of the judge and jury that they are so conditioned they will find the prisoner guilty and invoke the maximum penalty, whatever the circumstances of the crime, for they cannot do otherwise. That makes a mockery of reason and justice.

Equally, if I am a determinist, am I one because I cannot be an indeterminist? And if so, why argue the matter? Some people then have to be determinists, some indeterminists and, doubtless, others have to be agnostic or uninterested. And what is true of the belief in determinism should be true, on the determinist thesis, of all other beliefs, scientific or not. Does that make a mockery of truth and falsehood? Have they nothing to do with logic and evidence?

Well, we may be, individually, determined to believe only in propositions we think true because of evidence or analysis. But that brings another twist in the argument, in which belief is conditioned not just by nurture, but by good or bad reasoning. Of course, there is no reason whatever to think such determinism could hold only in matters of science. So there are people determined in matters of everyday belief to accept what is reasonable and reject what is unreasonable. Belief and action cease to be totally separate and impermeable; rather, they influence each other, on both the determinist and indeterminist theses. So people who choose reasonable beliefs, even if they do so in the most deterministic fashion, that is because they must, are likely to perform reasonable actions, not just respond to stimuli.

The argument has by now moved us from the causal nexus to the rational one. And that move changes everything. We can, I think, distinguish cause from reason, and say of people conditioned to be reasonable that, on occasions when they are indeed reasonable, they are not, in a physical sense, caused to do what they do, for what they do is based on logical patterns of thought, not on physical stimuli or past occurrences that have conditioned them. One aspect of the difference: causes are antecedent to acts, never subsequent, but purposes are both antecedent and subsequent, because *having* a purpose precedes the act, while the *content* of the purpose, an end-in-view, is an anticipation of an end which, when it actually occurs, succeeds it.

Let us continue to grant the determinist thesis, and apply it to reasons, not just causes. Then, if a man acts in terms of reasons, instead of causes, it is either because he must or because of antecedent events that can be stated mechanically. Perhaps he acts as he does because he was so conditioned by reading, formal study, teachers. Presumably he was differently conditioned before and did not act then in terms of reasons. The new conditioning, in overcoming the older conditioning, changed a person who acted unthinkingly, or with only psychological rationalization of his acts, into a person who acts as a result of reason and purpose. But that contradicts the determinist case, for it can be said properly, I think, that the new conditioning set our subject free in any legitimate sense of that word, even in the sense that he is sometimes undetermined.

Two things follow from applying determinism to itself and to reasons. First, if the determinist thesis is applied to the belief in determinism, we must either withdraw the claim that we believe it because it is true, since we may simply be determined to believe it, or we must accept the likelihood that men can be determined to be undetermined. That has already been shown. Second, much that happens in the life of the most reasonable and undetermined (or free) man is still a matter of causes, not reasons, for much in every life is unthinking and mechanical. And the most unthinking and determined man, if he is in possession of his faculties at all, will have some life that is a matter of reasons, not causes, for a modicum of logic and inner motivation exists in us all. So determinist (or behaviorist) explanation of human action may be of the greatest use, may even be necessary, in dealing with what is the result of causes, not reasons. Nothing is gained that I can see, even there, by adding the word "must" to an explanation of events. And determinism is impertinent, in two senses, in explanation of what is a result of reasons, not causes. It is only fair to add that the kind of explanation that is satisfactory in dealing with what is a result of reasons is unsatisfactory in dealing with what is a result of causes; it is then a conversion of purpose into teleology, of individual intent into what must be.

The principle of limited categories is quite sufficient, it seems to me, to refute the determinist case, by showing that determinism has generalized what may be "true within strict limitations" so that it has "a fallacious universality," and that determinism cannot state conceivable conditions under which it would be refuted, or indeed it would be refuted at once. The rest of the argument about determinism was an attempt to explore facets of a doctrine that is widely assumed, often implicitly and without examination, and that often leads to unreflective conclusions, some of which will next be examined.

CHAPTER TWO

Intellectual Perspectives

To continue the argument in greater detail and with other applications, what concerns me particularly is a tendency on the part of specialists to make pronouncements about man, morals, and society from the viewpoint of separate studies that deal with only one aspect of them. As it is, different schools of psychology have different ideas of man, as do the schools of sociology, economics, and political science. They would nevertheless all agree, however implicitly, on things that would be unacceptable to humanists. Among themselves humanists have the same sort of disagreements: man is a very different creature to a Victorian literary scholar than he is to a historian of the Elizabethan age.

The obvious, too-seldom-seen point already made quite fully, is that the conclusions about man and society reached by any one study of them are limited by the presuppositions, perspectives, or point of view, of the study, its exclusive categories. Economic man is of necessity "rational" and sociological man "irrational"; the first is constantly making decisions to further his advantage; the second is having things done to him. The first is constantly having to choose; the second is being socialized, molded, changed. I have overstated the case, of course, but the case is there, and because of it man and society seem different in the writings of economists and in the writings of sociologists. Yet no other difference is perhaps so great as the one between behavioral science (like sociology and some kinds of psychology) and most humanistic studies.

Society makes man what he is, as social science teaches, and we have learned much by applying that principle to human affairs. But man makes society what it is, as the humanities teach, and we can learn just as much—if different things—by applying that as a principle. We must not forget, either, that both principles are true. An old epistemological quandary is duplicated, but reversed, by much contemporary social science and psychology. We realize that if one starts a theory of knowledge with himself and his sensations alone, he can never in strict logic establish the existence of an external world; everything that happens can be accounted for as though it were an occurrence of sense data. Equally, if one starts a social science with society and social relations alone, or with observable human behavior, he can never really establish the existence of persons or selves, and everything that happens can be accounted for as though it were unintended, or a mechanical response to stimuli.

The social, as we usually treat it, is the realm of what happens to man, of the unanticipated consequences of his acts, of conditioning, socialization, and the environment. Since it contains no purpose or intent, it can be handled scientifically, like physical nature, without the embarrassment of teleological explanation. The humanistic, as we usually treat it, is the realm of purpose, of ethics, of the deliberate creation of ideas and things. (The political is both; it is an amalgam of the social and the humanistic.) Since the humanistic evidently contains purpose, it ordinarily falls outside the province of science, and because we repeatedly fail to distinguish the nature or quality of a humanistic event—the created idea or artifact, which is studied by humanists—from the conditions under which it was created—a proper topic for science—we rarely have a sound scientific account of the products of humanistic culture. I am not sure how useful such an account is, by itself, for it may consist of a statement about the history, society, politics, and economics of Florence in the fifteenth and sixteenth centuries, plus a biography of Ludovico Buonarroti and his wife, Francesca, and the rearing of their son, Michelangelo. Then one would need a humanistic account as well, of Michelangelo's accomplishment in sculpture and painting, before we could feel we understood Michelangelo at all. And someone should explain his Christian Platonism.

When, as specialists, we keep the two realms, the humanistic and the social, utterly separate, we tend to restrict purpose to the former alone and so make it impossible to deal fruitfully with an aspect of the social that affects all its parts, the moral. Purpose is irreducible in any total view of human action. As I have noted, scientific romanticism, fed on the triumphs of contemporary science, predicts a time in which all science, social as well as natural, can be stated in physico-chemical terms.* If that time ever comes, we will have a social science in which all the human qualities of man will be eliminated and he will be conceived, at least implicitly, as a more complicated termite. It is curious that all who attempt to treat man as though he were a machine must admit, if they raise the question at all, that this particular machine usually misconceives itself and is addicted, probably beyond cure, to discussing its mechanical responses in terms of consciousness, purpose, and ends.

There is no excuse for the scientist to try to treat other men as only physico-chemical beings or responders to stimuli, and to treat himself, as scientist, in any other way. Yet when scientists discuss scientific behavior, their topics include imagination, insight, theory-construction, and problem-solving, which sound for all the world like characteristics of minds, not machines. The activity of the scientist is, after all, intellectual: he creates a symbolic network, a frame of ideas, which he uses to make his subject matter intelligible and to allow him to predict, and sometimes even control. His scientific activity is highly purposive, it is in conformity with general ideas, and it is carefully directed. If he is a natural scientist, there is no real problem about the mental qualities of what he studies: he himself has intellectual traits, but his subject matter does not; he can treat it as mechanically as he likes. Yet some social scientists try to match the rigor of natural science, adopt its presuppositions, and treat their subject matter as though it did not have the characteristics of mind.**

Every one of those social scientists must know that his subject includes people like himself, and he may even understand that to mechanize man is as indefensible as to anthropomorphize machines, but he assumes he can apply the methods of the natural

*This has been enuniciated as a goal of natural and social scientists by a number of philosophers of science. A very readable statement is in Ernest Nagel's *The Structure of Science.*

**B. F. Skinner has tried to explain his own writing as only responses to stimuli—see his *Verbal Behavior*— but in doing so becomes untypically vague.

sciences only to materials as mechanical as theirs, and he insists on using only those methods because his scientific romanticism leads him to conceive himself as a kind of social physicist. Still his conclusions can be extremely valuable, so long as he remembers that his subject is not man *per se*.

The nub of the matter, perhaps, is that man is a moral agent or he is not fully man. And as a moral agent, man must be to some extent rational, for he must choose. No matter how the ideas and images of man have changed through history, no matter how varied they have been in different cultures, a definition of man that makes moral agency impossible to him renders him unrecognizable. A behaviorist might object to such ideas, insisting that the creature he studies is only a responder to stimuli and so cannot be a moral agent since he cannot, in effect, choose.* But that is like examining the component elements of water, asserting that they are gases, and concluding in the name of science that water is a gas and cannot, therefore, be wet. It is as clear that man is normally a moral being as that water is wet; it is an empirical fact, witnessed by all history, which may be explained, but cannot be explained away. The predicate, "moral," may need analysis but so, in a lesser way, may "wetness."

The point is not that our behaviorist proves man to be less than we thought him, but that the creature studied by the behaviorist is less than man, for he is man in only some of his functions or aspects, man in the artificial conditions of a laboratory, almost the "natural man" of an older political theory, whose observable responses are being studied. All that the extreme behaviorist is entitled to assert, then, is that what he studies—let us call it behavioristic man—is not a moral agent, or that the aspect of man revealed by his assumptions and methods does not include the attribute "moral." Splendid. There may be every reason to study man in those aspects and under those assumptions. But one's conclusions should then be restricted to one's subject matter.

Indeed, the very same conclusions may be correct if sufficiently restricted, yet false if unrestricted. When the scientist does not restrict his conclusions, he may have to falsify experience in order to defend his methods. He is then in the position of the

*Skinner says exactly that, in passages I shall examine later.

man who constructs an intelligence test and persuades Albert
Einstein to take it, only to discover that Einstein scores as a
low-grade moron; startled, yet convinced *a priori* of the accuracy of
a test which he should give up, he concludes that people have for
years, and with no scientific warrant, believed Einstein to be intelligent and gullibly accepted his theory of relativity.

All I am suggesting is that there is a *prima facie* case for
Einstein's intelligence. How do we make a test or scale for intelligence? By identifying intelligent men and finding their relevant
traits. Thus the "scientific" test that shows Einstein to be a moron
is *prima facie* a bad test. Equally, human life and society are
saturated in morality and its problems, and to deny the very existence of moral agency, or to "explain" it out of existence, only
reveals the error in the mode of explanation. Is fighting a war only
a matter of diplomacy and military decision? Is obedience to law
only prudence? These are moral issues at bottom, and we behave
as though they were, whatever our verbal denials.

What one sees depends of course on what one is looking at,
how he is looking at it, and what he is looking for. The social
scientist looks at institutions, processes, and groups to find their
structure and function and their effects on man. The humanist
looks at individual artifacts, like documents and works of art, to
find their structure and meaning, and at personal and institutional
response, to find their effects on society. The man writing a book
finds almost everything he reads grist to his mill. So to the social
scientist it is obvious that when conditions are ripe for a discovery
or invention, it will be made. Somebody was bound to sail to
America in the fifteenth or sixteenth century; Columbus happened to. Somebody was bound to invent the telephone at almost
the time Bell, in fact, did. Again and again, different people discovered the same thing at about the same time quite independently. The evidence seems so overwhelming that few people are
concerned about the possibility that some things were never discovered at all, though the supposed conditions for discovery
existed, or the probability that other things were not discovered
the first time that conditions were ripe (perhaps we can know that
to be the case only when the same things were discovered later
under similar conditions). Determinism thus slips into history.

The question of discovery has implications for other problems about man, the importance of the individual in history, his

influence on his society, the difference to the future made by the fact of his existence. Answers to these problems are too often presupposed, not discussed. If somebody would surely do what in fact Columbus or Bell did, at about the time they did it, then the very existence of the two would, supposedly, make no difference to posterity. If a scientist knew enough of the social, economic, political, and intellectual conditions of the times just before the discoveries of Columbus or Bell, he could presumably have predicted that someone would act as they did, and been proved correct even if Columbus and Bell had died at birth.

The argument seems to run thus: science states the conditions under which events occur; if we know that under conditions C, event E occurs, we assume that if we actually observe an instance of C, it will be followed by an instance of E. How could such reasoning fail to apply to human history? Under certain conditions, discovery and invention take place, and the same is true of all other human behavior. So an excellent study of revolutions concludes that revolutions occur when bad conditions have recently improved and later it seems that the improvement will be checked or destroyed.* The evidence comes from studies of particular revolutions. Now let us assume the best possible—and so, most improbable—case: all known revolutions have been studied, and all have occurred under just these conditions. The evidence would seem overwhelming, and we would feel entitled to conclude that if the Gracchi, Spartacus, Lenin, or any other revolutionary leaders had not existed, others would have taken their places, and the revolutions would have arrived on schedule.

Yet just this conclusion is dubious. After all, the study of revolution did not focus on occasions on which C was discovered, always to be followed by E, a revolution. It focused on occurrences of E, and discovered that all instances of E were preceded by instances of C. And that is quite another matter, for there might have been many instances in history of the presumed conditions for revolution which were not in fact followed by revolution, many C's not followed by E's. And that would mean that the conditions discovered by the study are not really the conditions of revolution at all, or more likely, are only some of them.

*James C. Davies: "Toward a Theory of Revolution," *American Sociological Review,* February, 1962.

Unfortunately, this study of revolution is not a solitary instance of a flaw in method in which some conditions for the occurrence of an event are elevated to causal status; it is fairly common. So we must look for the root of the error. That is to be found, I think, in the implicit philosophy of social science (held by many behavioralists and others seeking a social physics) which includes the belief that causation in history and society is entirely a matter of general social conditions. Thus the conditions that seemed relevant to revolution in this study are poverty, oppression, exploitation, status, and mobility. When such conditions are of a given kind, revolution presumably occurs.

This pattern, of course, is derived from natural science, and our implicit social philosophy contains the assumption that social phenomena can be explained, and explained only, by patterns of the sort that provide explanation of natural phenomena. The very statement that revolutions *occur* under certain conditions reveals that assumption. Otherwise one would say that revolutions are *made* under those conditions. And that is a very different statement, for it makes the conditions at most necessary, and leads to questions about those who make revolutions. What kind of people revolted—perhaps some kinds with certain qualities and traditions do revolt in such circumstances and other kinds do not? Who are the leaders of revolt? Perhaps men of a particular character, or charisma, or articulateness are needed, and without them no revolution takes place, only disorder, if even that. These are humanistic categories, too often excluded from social science.

The typical bias of the sort of social scientist I am discussing is revealed here by the kinds of conditions he thinks relevant. A historian who is a humanist at heart might look for different conditions, human factors exclusively, thus revealing his assumption that men make history—a correct assumption, but a bias in this case, because it is also true that history makes men. The humanist, like the social scientist, easily develops his bias by the very nature of the things he studies. Different conclusions seem to, and sometimes do, follow from the same questions asked about different kinds of creation. As the scientist "knows" that the state of mathematical knowledge was such in the latter half of the seventeenth century that the integral calculus would have been invented by someone, whether or not his name was Newton or Leibniz, the humanist knows that if the *St. Matthew's Passion* had not been composed by Johann Sebastian Bach it would never have been composed at all. There would, the scientist assumes, have been a telephone even if there had never been an Alexander Graham Bell. But that is less sure than that there would not have been a *Divine Comedy* had there not been Dante.

To correct a narrowness of assumption that vitiates many conclusions, the social scientist and the humanist must use each other's viewpoints and categories. As one instance: to the scientific mind the seaworthiness of ships, the improvement in navigation, and the demand for certain products made it a foregone conclusion that someone would "discover" America and bring knowledge of it back to Europe. The humanist mind is concerned with the vision and courage of Columbus. As to the inportance of the individual in history, it might seem to the scientist that it would make no difference if Columbus or another sailor had made the voyage and brought the report. But if not Columbus, with his vision, energy, persuasiveness, and luck, would anyone have found America in *1492*? If the discoverer came later, *would he have sailed under the flag of Spain*? If the answer to both these questions is no, it is likely that the history of the world would have been quite different.

It seems obvious to many educated people that when the time is "ripe" for anything, discovery, invention, war, or revolution, that thing will occur. It seems obvious, also, that the men and women who *bring* the change are only *bearers* of it, for if they did not do what they did, someone else would. And all this turns out to be false, at least as a generalization. It is a deterministic or quasi-deterministic view of history in which the "ripeness" of conditions is a stimulus that must yield an appropriate response. And it can beg all questions. If one asks whether anyone but Beethoven could have written the Ninth Symphony at that time, under those conditions, the answer has to be that nobody else could, but that is qualified by the comment that Beethoven had to. And why? Because he was Beethoven, and Beethoven was so conditioned. But clearly, had Beethoven died before he wrote the Ninth Symphony, there would not have been that music. Further, reflection on the argument so far should show that, although Beethoven did write the Ninth Symphony, he might not have, even though he lived long enough.

Some people are less exercised by the errors of such specialization, errors that result from over-generalization, when dealing
with serious issues that elude specialization than they are by the
unimportance of many conclusions that are true. As in R. B.
Perry's old definition, we learn more and more about less and less
until we may know everything about nothing. Dissatisfaction with
specialization as the royal or only road to knowledge sometimes
results in a demand for interdisciplinary studies in order to avoid
the proliferation of trivia. This has created major academic crises,
for a number of years, with much heat, little light, and extremely
strong feelings on both sides. The specialist regards interdisciplinary studies as entirely a teaching device, incapable of discovery, limited to organization of what is already known, and perhaps
obscuring that by mingling what is known in several fields of
knowledge, to the confusion of all of them. The scientist and the
scholar, the specialist believes, can only function in a limited area
or discipline; the interdisciplinary teacher is only a teacher and
cannot even be a good teacher because he is nothing else. As for
the scientist or scholar who tries to teach in an interdisciplinary
way, he either does not know enough, because of his specialized
training or, if he takes the time and has the ability to learn
enough, he falls behind in his specialty and is no longer a scholar
or scientist.

But the interdisciplinarian insists that real problems are never
specialized, that specialized problems are often trivia, and that the
relevance of science and scholarship to life and society requires
more than specialization. He advocates both specialization and the
interdisciplinary while his opponent wants only specialization.

Unfortunately, neither party to this quarrel has analyzed the
interdisciplinary sufficiently to make clear what it is. It is not, or
at least should not be, the addition of one discipline or subject
—those words are used interchangeably by most writers on the
subject, and distinctions are thus further blurred—to another, so
that they are considered either together or *seriatim*. It is not just a
matter of relation and influence of one subject to another, important though that is. The interdisciplinary is, at its best, a subject-
matter defined by a set of categories divisible into sub-sets, each
of which also defines a subject-matter, or is part of another subject-matter.

Not all combinations of category sets are necessarily viable. As those of chemistry and magic made alchemy, those of physics and ethics may make an equally absurd non-subject. But just as categories of biology and chemistry are combined in biochemistry, so categories from other fields of study may make valid new fields. History and sociology may combine to make historical sociology; anthropology and ethics, psychology and politics, jurisprudence, history, sociology, and ethics may all make new and vital subjects. And as new subjects exist, in which discoveries can be made, knowledge classified and organized, and laws formulated, their practitioners can be scientists and scholars, specialists who are not narrow, interdisciplinary students whose subjects are not thin.

My guess is that when the principle of limited categories is violated consistently a new subject-matter is desired, although it has not yet been created. Failure to add categories from other subjects makes conclusions untenable, because they apply to a subject larger than is legitimate in virtue of the categories employed. The most difficult combinations of categories are perhaps those which involve both social science and the humanities, yet just those combinations may be most rewarding.

How else can we deal with countless important questions that have been all but neglected up to now. For instance, under what conditions do the great periods of art occur: Athenian and Elizabethan drama, High Renaissance painting and sculpture, baroque music? How can we explain the emergence and disappearance of great and distinctive styles? What are the relations between styles of civilization and styles of art? Under what conditions does a nation concentrate on one art rather than another? To answer such questions we must know a good deal about the art whose conditions we seek. And we must know even more about art if we rely on it to reveal cultural beliefs and values, as we do in the case of preliterate peoples.

What can we do in physical or mechanical or social terms alone to explain how Shakespeare came to write *King Lear*? Perhaps we can explain in those terms how he came to write, and even how he came to write poetic drama (although I doubt it), but the terms are surely inadequate to explain why Shakespeare wrote *Lear*, or why he wrote *As You Like It* but did not write *The Knight of the Burning Pestle*.

If we were to generalize this limitation on explanation in physical or social terms, we might say that even if we could explain a man acting in some way we could not explain his performing an act with the special qualities of that act, especially when the act is "creative"—in art, in science, in morals, in philosophy, etc. This would be true of any determinist or reductionist thesis. For instance, if one could explain in sociological terms the flowering of English dramatic poetry in the age of Elizabeth, he still could not explain the form of Elizabethan drama without its historic development, which requires more than physical and social terms, and he could not explain the particulars and qualities of *Doctor Faustus* at all, which require aesthetic and literary criticism. Insofar as we can "explain" *Doctor Faustus,* we have to deal with the form of the play, its background in medieval legend, the linguistic usage of the late sixteenth century in England, Marlowe's imagination, and the internal structure of the play, the relations of incidents, characters, and images.

It is not necessary, although it may be rewarding, to construct entirely new "sciences" in any formal way to deal with questions that transcend the "sciences" we already have. Every subject matter has its own categories which are used as the key terms of investigation and analysis. We know we are reading sociology when we encounter "status," "role," "stratification," "social mobility," and the like, as we know we are reading economics when we encounter "market," "supply," "demand," "marginal utility," and so on. Categories such as these can occasionally be used in a subject other than the one from which they came, but then they must be absorbed into the other viewpoint, related to a new set of categories, if they are to be genuinely useful. The same phenomenon is often examined within different intellectual disciplines, and so from different points of view or sets or categories. That is all to the good, and the man who can see the phenomenon from a variety of viewpoints sees it more fully, like the man who walks around a statue, instead of gazing at it fixedly from only one spot. The limits of specialization emerge quickly when one insists that this point of view alone reveals the truth about the phenomenon, that the point from which he views the statue is the only right place from which to look.

I shall treat three examples, two of them briefly, of the

fixed viewpoint which distorts the view. The eminent sociologist of knowledge, Karl Mannheim, wrote: "Strictly speaking, it is incorrect to say that the single individual thinks. Rather it is more correct to insist that he participates in thinking further what other men have thought before him."* Those other men, one supposes, also participated in thinking further, *ad infinitum.* And all of them thought "further," not differently. In categories other than Mannheim's—nature and mind, for example—it is clear that only "the single individual" thinks. To be sure, if one's viewpoint and terms are entirely social, human nature disappears and so, perhaps, does mind. By that time the person is gone, too, and without that idea one might find himself talking like Mannheim. But if one retains the human animal in his viewpoint as well as the social creature, it is easy enough to conclude that each man uses the language of his culture and inherits many of its beliefs and values, without being pushed into the grotesque idea that those beliefs and values come from some collective thought, issued as though by a joint thought company. For a man does not "participate" with others in an act of thought which is jointly theirs; he thinks.

Mannheim's direction, if not his idea, is relatively clear: he is reducing as close to zero as possible what is natural in man, so that only the social survives. If he were a better writer, he might say what F. H. Bradley did, but mean it literally: ". . . man is a social being; he is real only because he is social . . ." Mannheim's categories are social and historical. They make man entirely a creature of culture, time, and circumstance. Another current viewpoint makes man timeless, and hardly more than a bundle of responses to stimuli. The categories of behaviorist psychology and of laboratory control have led B. F. Skinner to the belief that in man there is no originating control beneath the skin. In consequence, he has decided that choice is illusory and, that being the case, the very word "responsibility" is meaningless; men will just have to learn to do without it. I suspect that lawyers, nations, associations, and individual men in their relations with other men will always be unable to do without it. How uncooperative they are with "science."

Mr. Skinner should be taken very seriously, though, and for

*_Ideology and Utopia,_ New York, Harcourt, Brace, 1936, p. 3.

good reason: he is a first-rate psychologist, an extraordinarily ingenious experimenter, fertile in ideas, clear in his writing, and
rigorous in pursuing his own idea of psychology to its consequences. It is those consequences that are important for our argument, for they openly reject morality, responsibility, freedom, and
obligation. Even if today's young psychologists do not follow Mr.
Skinner so avidly as they once did, his mark is on many of them.

In explaining his own "radical behaviorism" and its relation
to other studies of man, Mr. Skinner wrote:

> The Freudian emphasis on the role of the irrational
> was offensive: but although Freud was a determinist certain
> controlling forces remained within man himself, no matter
> how unworthy they may have seemed. The crowning blow
> to the apparent sovereignty of man came with the shift of
> attention to the external determiners of action. The social
> sciences and psychology reached this stage at about the same
> time. Whenever some feature of the environment—past or
> present—is shown to have an effect on human conduct, the
> fancied contribution of the individual himself is reduced.
> The program of a radical behaviorism left no originating con-
> trol inside the skin.*

There is nothing to be alarmed at in this; rather it is occasion for rejoicing. Man's power may grow as a result, Skinner
thinks, although I suspect it is only power to control animals and
power for men to manipulate each other for the sake of ends that
cannot be justified.

In any event, Skinner says:

> There is no reason why scientific methods cannot now
> be applied to the study of man himself—to practical prob-
> lems of society and, above all, to the behavior of the individ-
> ual. We must not turn back because the prospect suddenly
> becomes frightening. The truth may be strange, and it may
> threaten cherished beliefs, but as the history of science
> shows, the sooner a truth is faced, the better. No scientific
> advance has ever actually damaged man's position in the

Verbal Behavior, Appleton-Century-Crofts, Inc., 1957, pp. 458f.

world. It has merely characterized it in a different way. Indeed, each achievement has in a sense *increased* the role which men play in the scheme of things. If we eventually give a plausible account of human behavior as part of a lawfully determined system, man's power will increase even more rapidly. Men will never become originating centers of control, because their behavior will itself be controlled, but their role as mediators may be extended without limit. The technological applications of such a scientific achievement cannot now be fathomed. It is difficult to foresee the verbal adjustments which will have to be made. "Personal freedom" and "responsibility" will make way for other bywords which, as is the nature of bywords, will probably prove satisfying enough.*

The scientific methods now to be applied to man himself are—the language makes it evident—the methods, in general, that have been applied to nature. The science of man becomes part of the science of nature, and man cannot be allowed traits that are not part of a "lawfully determined system," emphasis really on "determined."

Of course, we live in and respond to a world, but do we do nothing else but respond, even after we are formed and reasonably mature? Some new behaviorists may say yes, we also respond to inner tensions and glandular-chemical stimuli. But that's the same bag of tricks, elaborated, for it still denies an inner life, reflection, and imagination. And Skinner uses reductionist words casually, a matter in which he is not, unfortunately, alone. "Personal freedom" and "responsibility" are "bywords," which suggests they stand for nothing. The awful intellectual and emotional wrench, the anguish, and even the suicide one may suffer if such cherished beliefs are taken away by "science" is reduced to "verbal adjustments."

What is apparently intolerable to social scientists like Skinner (of course, in their private lives almost all of them know better, one hopes) is the existence of a contemplative and private thinker. Utter intolerance does not reveal itself in imprisoning such men, as some countries do, but in denying their existence, as in Orwell's

*Ibid., pp. 459 f.

1984 enemies of the state are not just killed, but all records of their lives destroyed. Again a distinction between appearance and reality is drawn, and though a Nietzsche *seems* to come on his explosive aphorisms by reflection, we are assured implicitly that he is *really* only responding to stimuli, external, genetic, or chemical. Of course, none of this is proven; it is a way dear to some scientific hearts of explaining complex phenomena simply. And it seems impossible to shake a crusading faith in this mode of explanation, for it is a faith no weaker than Islam.

Skinner was impelled to write what I have quoted as a response to a conversation with Alfred North Whitehead. But he did not meet objections to claims like his that Whitehead had voiced long before. Whitehead said, of what he called "physiologists" in the 1920's:

> ... the trained body of physiologists under the influence of ideas germane to their successful methodology entirely ignore the whole mass of adverse evidence. We have here a colossal example of anti-empirical dogmatism arising from a successful methodology. Evidence which lies outside the method simply does not count.*

To detail the sort of thing he means, Whitehead continues:

> There is clear evidence that certain operations of certain animal bodies depend upon the foresight of an end and the purpose to attain it. It is no solution to the problem to ignore this evidence because other operations have been explained in terms of physical and chemical laws. The existence of a problem is not even acknowledged. It is vehemently denied. Many a scientist has patiently designed experiments for the *purpose* of substantiating his belief that animal operations are motivated by no purpose. He has perhaps spent his spare time in writing articles to prove that human beings are as other animals so that 'purpose' is a category irrelevant for the explanation of their bodily activities, his own activities included. Scientists animated by the purpose

---

*The Function of Reason, Beacon Press, 1967, p. 15. The book contains Whitehead's Vanuxem Foundation Lectures at Princeton University, March 19, 1929.

of proving that they are purposeless constitute an interesting subject for study.*

Purpose, as I said, is irreducible in human life. Without it, a man is not even a mouse, for a mouse may have purpose, but something still lower on the evolutionary scale, and perhaps not on the scale at all. I can see no genuine account of the moral life without purpose. But there is surely no plausible account at all without the obligatory "ought" and, like too many philosophers, many behaviorists reduce that to something utterly outside of morals. Skinner, for one, does, in this passage:

> Responses to variables often appear as statements of "purpose" or "meaning"...*I am looking for my glasses* appears to include a response to the object of the speaker's behavior, but how can an object with which the speaker is not yet in contact control a verbal response? Such behavior must be regarded as equivalent to *When I have behaved in this way in the past, I have found my glasses and have then stopped behaving in this way,* or *Circumstances have arisen in which I am inclined to emit any behavior which in the past has led to the discovery of my glasses; such behavior includes the behavior of looking in which I am now engaged.* It is not some purposive character of the behavior itself which the individual thus tacts,** but the variables in control of the behavior. Similarly, responses to controlling variables often include the forms *ought* or *should.* Some instances of *I ought to go* may be translated *Under these circumstances I generally go, If I go I shall be handsomely reinforced,* or *If I go I shall be released from the threat of censure for not going.* (Skinner's italics.)

It is hard to do justice to this statement. But one must make some comments. "How can an object with which the speaker is not yet in contact control a verbal response?" Skinner asks. One

---

Ibid., p. 16.

**Op. cit.*, pp. 144f. Mr. Skinner invented the word "tact" in this use, as a kind of contraction of "makes contact with" the physical world. "A tact may be defined as a verbal operant in which a response of given form is evoked (or at least strengthened) by a particular object or event or property of an object or event." (pp. 81f.)

thinks of a young couple about to build their first house, talking happily and constantly about what it will be like to live in it. Their "contact" with it is, of course, imagination: they have a very good idea of what it will be like when finished. But no. Skinner regards the obvious as impossible and wants to talk only about past behavior (which did not include building a house). One wonders, in thinking of Skinner's own example, about the man who for the first time mislays his first glasses.

But it is the translation of "ought" that explicitly omits the moral. Having done away with purpose and meaning, Skinner then translated "ought" into habit, reward, or punishment, the meaning of his last three statements. Suppose we ask of the first of the three: Why do I generally go under these circumstances? I can have no purpose in mind, according to this account. Assume the answer is that I go now because I habitually go. Then how did I acquire such a habit? We are pushed back to the last two state-ments. I shall be reinforced (rewarded) or censured (punished). One wonders a little ruefully how far all this science is from the famous sentence Jeremy Bentham printed in 1780 and Helvetius in French before him: "Nature has placed mankind under the govern-ance of two sovereign masters, pain and pleasure." Bentham at least thought that morality could be based on this principle, for he continued: "It is for them alone to point out what we ought to do, as well as to determine what we shall do." Skinner has no such interest.

We still have to ask about the last passage quoted from Skinner why I should be reinforced if I go or threatened with censure if I don't. In the Skinnerian scheme whoever reinforces or censures me can have no purpose in mind. Can he justify his behavior by its moral significance? Clearly not. So far as I can tell, he is manipulating me in these ways because of his own past experience, and the ways in which he may be rewarded or punished for his treatment of me. After all, the type of explana-tion that is given my conduct must be given his. So no man is in the web of morality, nor does he act with purpose, with ends-in-view.

Can one go farther in minimizing man? Yes. Kenneth R. Minogue, for instance, in his book *The Liberal Mind* finds that entities like society and church exist, but writes of "the liberal invention of the individual," making individual man a political idea that lacks reality. Mr. Minogue will not want to go much farther, but people have thought that termites, so tight is their society, should not be conceived as individual existents, but rather as organs of the whole, the termitorium. Merely because they are not physically connected to each other, we need not assume that they have more individual existence than my finger, which is indeed connected to my body, but exists only as a part of that body. If such a thing is true of termites, why not of men? There are at least suggestions of such an idea.

To return for those suggestions to the giants of contemporary social science in America, let us consider the most famous of our sociologists (who, as a younger man, believed quite the opposite of what I shall quote from him). In a review of a book by Robert Cooley Angell, Talcott Parsons, the dean of American sociology, went further in some ways than Mannheim or Skinner in reducing man to less than he seems. He made this criticism: "The difficulty seems to rest in Angell's tendency to hypostatize the individual and endow him with a kind of total status. With the intricate structural differentiation of American society, however, this becomes increasingly unrealistic. It is not so much the individual who is or is not morally integrated in the society, but a relational structure which is relatively more or less well integrated through the institutionalization of its norms."* The word "hypostatize" as used here seems synonymous with "reify," to treat an abstraction as if it were a thing. Mr. Parsons may, then, be contending that individuals are abstractions and "relational structures" are things, or that people are not individuals, but relational (social) structures. A fascinating suggestion, but not one based on a large view of man and society. Curiously, this situation is understood as the result of social change: it was apparently once more realistic (or less unrealistic) to treat people as entities. Now new categories are appropriate, presumably because of "the intricate structural differentiation" of society. But are not these categories then used without limitation to characterize man himself and his social world, to imply, for example, almost (actually?) the nonexistence of persons, at least as we have known them?

---

*The American Journal of Sociology, September 1959, p. 226.

More recently, Mr. Parsons has expanded his use of the word "actor," which he had once used to refer to "individual human beings as personalities in roles." Now "... 'actor' can refer to a business firm in interaction with a household, or, at the cultural level, the implementation of empirical beliefs."* This definition, of course, is part of a theory of society as "action systems" in which an "act" is "the logically minimal unit of analysis." The unit act consists of an actor and a situation, and the actor may be, we are told, an implementation of belief. At the least, this seems a poor choice of words, but whatever else it means, it is probably a further movement toward rejection of the person as an individual entity, or even a basic element in the social process. Equally it is a rejection of the importance of reason for society—though not for science—because *men* are capable of reason and sometimes behave rationally in social affairs, but *actors* only play roles, and *implementations* cannot think.

Now, it is one thing to suppose that sociology is properly concerned with institutions, patterns, interactive units, social processes and systems, but not with individuals, because matters of purpose, motive, and consciousness must be minimized in dealing with statistical aggregates. In that case, we choose our categories to fit our subject, and limit our conclusions accordingly. But it is another thing entirely to suggest that people do not, as individuals, think (Mannheim), that they are not, as individuals, real entities (Parsons); and that no one of them, as an individual, is of any importance to the social process (the argument about discovery and invention). This is to direct one's thought by his categories but to broaden his conclusions to matters that do not come under those categories. It is as if a physicist pointed out, for the purposes of physics, that men must be treated under the categories of mass and energy, and concluded that what could be said of men in those terms was all that could be truly said of them. Too often one finds a scientist, whose professional life is thought, deciding that thought does little or nothing in the world, and one is then reminded of Lord Lindsay's dictum: "If social theory is to be like physics, its elements must be identical atoms."

American Sociological Review, August 1960, p. 467.

As for "role" and "actor," words so important in current sociology, it may be worth noting that the ancient Greek used the equivalent of the word "hypocrisy" for "role," and "hypocrite" for "actor." Is there an implication, as "actor" and "role" are used today, that the parts we play in society belie our persons and are rehearsed portrayals of what is expected, but not of what we are? Or is it assumed we are nothing but the roles we play, and that under the actor's mask there is no face? The language of "actor" and "role" can be borrowed successfully from the theater only as men act parts they did not create on a social stage they did not design. And that is the world of sociology, not of society. The point cannot be made too sharply. Man may be treated as actor and his conduct as role, his very being may be subordinated to social relationships, if and only if the context is that of sociology. If it is, then we are entitled to discuss man as though he were not guided by reason and purpose, and we can treat him as not fully real, for sociological man is not real man. He is an abstraction created for scientific purposes. ("Real man," too, is an idea, but an idea based on all relevant categories of nature, society, and person.) I suspect, or at least hope, that whatever plausibility we find in such accounts of "man" derives from an implicit recognition that the subject is sociological man, i.e., man as understood under the categories of sociological thought.

What is most misleading here, even absurd, is that the ordinary definition of sociology as the study of society and the implicit definition of society as the world of human action, bring sociologists to identify man himself with their abstraction. Of course, political scientists and economists often treat man as entirely rational, equally forgetting the special context in which they place him. And, as I have argued, neo-behaviorists in psychology sometimes forget the nature and limits of their science, which they may think of as *the* study of human behavior, when they characterize man entirely in terms of their findings. But the commonness of this error does not mitigate it, and it may influence the educated layman most when it is found in subjects so popular as sociology or so influential as psychology. Man can be of only dubious consequence to himself or society if he is identified totally with sociological or behavioristic man, for man as stage actor or responder is not man as moral agent. The latter, but not the former, involves reason fully, and must be thought of under the categories of choice, decision, and responsibility.

CHAPTER THREE

A Preface to Morals

Criteria of meaning, such as operationism* or verifiability, are often applied more widely than they should be, just as the conclusions of some sciences are. The very statement of the criterion is usually misleading, as is the use of the word "meaning." The only genuine test that a statement has meaning is that people understand it, and the proof of understanding is that one can say or do things as a result of it. What happens too frequently is that one understands a statement but is told that it is meaningless—at least cognitively meaningless—because it does not conform to some criterion, such as that it must be testable, at least in principle. The fear of the Lord may be the beginning of wisdom but to say so may easily provoke the charge that one is talking nonsense. And to avoid such statement for fear that it is nonsense is to develop a trained incapacity for understanding whatever is not obvious.

The principle of limited categories can be useful as a guide when one is considering criteria of meaning, because most criteria have been formulated with natural science as a model. Operationism, for example, so important to social scientists, was formulated by the Nobel Prize-winning physicist Percy Bridgman for use in natural science. Such criteria are themselves models of scientific discourse, not descriptions of what scientists do. But models are expanded metaphors, and are not to be taken literally, so even within natural science meaning criteria may be, and have

---

*Operationism reduces all meaning to the human operations necessary to test its truth. Thus the meaning of a statement that a building is x storeys high is the counting of the storeys. In consequence, what seems to be a statement about a building becomes a statement about ourselves.

been, too rigid. Outside natural science there is little reason to use meaning criteria based on natural science, although they may be heuristic, cautioning us against absurd utterance. The proper limitation to the application of operationism or the verifiability criterion should lead to such assertions, at most, as that a given statement could not be accepted fully as yet, in the body of natural science because it violates the criterion, but may not be cast out of science as its content may be suggestive or useful.

Moral discourse can be irresponsible or, like anything else, meaningless, but not because it violates criteria that forbid its acceptance as natural science, which it clearly is not. "Honesty is the best policy" is sometimes false; "Thou shalt not kill" is meaningless if we demand verification by observation. And the patterns of natural science, as I have argued, should not be rigidly adhered to even by the social sciences, because the difference made to society and history by an individual can be important, and the subject matter of social science is not unreasoning matter but rational creatures capable of voluntary action. Moral discourse, with its "ought" and "ought not," is partly outside all science, but that does not mean it is necessarily capricious or unrigorous, any more than statutory law is, or a legal brief. I shall try to show later how morals should enter into, or be used by social science.

Yet one principle, widely accepted at the moment, holds that moral discourse cannot be a serious intellectual enterprise because "ought" cannot be derived from "is," that is, that statements of duty and obligation cannot be based on statements of fact. That all men honor their parents is, clearly, insufficient for the conclusion that they ought to, and the contradictory assertion, that some men do not honor their parents, is just as insufficient as the basis for a moral judgment. However, when I say, "X is right; therefore you ought to do it," the argument is valid if it means "Everyone ought to do x; therefore you ought to do it." "Ought" is in the premise and so is entitled to be in the conclusion. But where do I get the initial proposition containing "ought"? Not from factual propositions alone, because they yield no conclusions containing "ought," and not from still other propositions containing "ought," because that would lead to infinite regression.

The entire argument assumes the prior rejection of traditional ethics, with its postulate of an ultimate moral base (like
God, Nature, or Reason) or a *summum bonum* (like pleasure or
self-fulfillment). For the moral skeptic—I think we are entitled to
call him that—can go only so far in making this argument against
traditional ethics, and then must shift his ground. When the traditional moralist says, "God commands us (or "It is in conformity
with Nature or Reason") to do x; therefore we ought to do x,"
the skeptic can point to an implicit major premise, "We ought to
do what God commands" (or "We ought to do what is in conformity with Nature or Reason"). And why, the skeptic can ask,
ought we to do it? If the answer is another proposition containing
"ought" we can still ask why and there will be infinite regress.

So far as I can see, this is as far as the skeptic can go in
dealing with traditional ethics without shifting his ground, because
the traditional moralist can ask what in the world the skeptic
thinks "ought" means. Its basic meaning, he can add, is what God
commands (or what is in conformity with Nature or Reason, or
what leads to pleasure or self-fulfillment). The skeptic's new
ground, cogent enough for its purpose, is that he can find no way
to discover what God commands, etc., or why pleasure or self-fulfillment should be the highest good. But that is an old criticism
and one of a very different kind from the question of "is" and
"ought." What is significant for the "is-ought" argument is the
question what is meant by that "ought" which presumably cannot
be derived from "is." I shall come to that a little later.

The contention that "ought" cannot be derived from "is" is
an unfortunate way of establishing a new subject, Meta-Ethics, or
Ethical Analysis. Its categories are exclusively those of logical and
linguistic analysis, and its subject is moral—and perhaps legal—
codes and ethical statements, not conduct, but what is *said* about
conduct. The categories of moral discourse—evaluations, precepts,
imperatives, rules, duties, obligations—are not included in the categories of Ethical Analysis, but the statements resulting from the
use of the categories of moral discourse become the subject matter
of Ethical Analysis. Rarely does Ethical Analysis violate the principle of limited categories. It has its own warrant and *raison
d'être.* But Ethical Analysis is usually justified by the "ought-is"
argument, or something like it, which eliminates moral discourse as

an intellectual enterprise, and so Ethical Analysis apes science in divesting its subject matter of the element of rationality. Ethical Analysis needs no more justification than other subjects, namely, that something can be learned or clarified, and its curious justification is illicit reductionism in the most fundamental of human concerns.

Fewer people today than in the 1930s and 1940s believe that the only meaning to be assigned the moral "ought" is preference or taste, but it is instructive to ask why such an idea was and is believed, for the same reasons are still offered in support of other forms of moral skepticism and reductionism. The contention is that the statement "One ought to do x" means "I prefer x, so I would like you to prefer x, too." Of course that you should prefer anything because I do is sheer non sequitur, and to suppose that people really mean anything of this sort when they say "One ought to do x" is to assume they are all foolish and arrogant. So the philosophers (Rudolf Carnap, for example, and other logical empiricists) who reduce the moral to the psychological in this fashion do not appeal to ordinary usage but to science, indeed to the patterns of explanation in natural science, which they assume as the type of all explanation.*

Moral statements, the argument runs, are not as they stand testable by scientific procedure and so are meaningless unless translated into another form, which is testable. To say "I prefer x" or "I should like you to prefer x" is testable, at least in principle, by observation of my behavior and, perhaps, by experiment. If, in answer, one pressed the point that the translation might be testable but was no longer a moral statement, the response might be agreement, an agreement based on the idea that there can be no meaningful moral statements at all. One presupposition of all this is that whatever cannot enter the body of science, conceived on the model of natural science, can have no genuine meaning, whether it be called morality or poetry, religion

*The meaning criteria of Logical Empiricism were so rigid as to lead often to unwarranted reductionism. Carnap used to say that the sentence "This is a book about Africa" meant only "This book contains the word 'Africa'," But the book might be a system of metaphysics, in which "Africa" was used in an example. Scarcely a book *about* Africa!

or metaphysics. That presupposition was made explicit and defended fully by logical positivists. But another presupposition was understood less, and so was more insidious.

Morality, it was assumed by positivists, cultural relativists in anthropology, and many others, was a body of statements or rules of conduct intellectually defensible by argument and test, or it was nothing. No other alternative was possible. We are guided in life by the conventions of our society, to which we are habituated or conditioned, but they are no more than conventions because other societies and other ages have, and had, their conventions, too, and there can be no scientific way of deciding that some are right and others wrong, some better and some worse. Since the conventions of each society provide some necessary uniformity of conduct, perhaps morality is unnecessary. When confronted with conventions they found unpleasant, some philosophers spoke of preferring those that had survived for years and seemed to work. But that was only their preference, not a criterion of morality.

I suspect that the word "convention" caused trouble because it was used by men very familiar with conventions in a logical or mathematical system. But a social convention is something else again; it may be manners, but it may also be morals. We are not entitled simply to assume that conventional morality is no morality at all; it is the morality in which we live, and breathe, act, suffer, and die. I shall discuss it further in the next chapter. Here I want to insist that the very use of the word "conventional" is misleading. Because conventions in a logical system are stipulated, social conventions should not, by analogy, be thought of as decided arbitrarily. Conventional morals arise in the course of group and institutional history; and neither history nor the institutional arrangements of any society are sheer accident.

The moral skeptic asserts that facts have no ethical significance, that they are related to other facts in a physical order but that they are entirely adventitious, unconnected, to a moral order. To be sure, the facts, or phenomena, of astronomy provide the skeptic with a good instance. But what about the phenomena of history, the results of human activity, which is motivated and purposive? It is not reasonable, as it is in the case of astronomy, to deny any connection with the moral. Social phenomena result in part from moral concern, reflection, and indoctrination. The moral has been involved in human choice, in human conflict, in peace and war. Is it not, therefore, necessary for the skeptic's case to assume that conventional, or existent, moral arrangements are irrelevant to morality? And doesn't such an assumption rest on a presupposition that man's activity is only mechanical response to external factors, although—since he can think of moral matters—his mind is creative? At this point I think the argument becomes absurd. It is one thing to discover that conventional morality is not identical with critical morality*—an important and liberating discovery. It is quite another thing, and most implausible, to contend that conventional existent morality is unconnected with morality in any reasonable sense of that word.

Two extreme attitudes toward history, supporting different political beliefs, are equally misleading. One may be thought of as a liberal, or radical, belief that history is brute fact, purely adventitious, or the result of unthinking social forces which make institutions an embodiment of chance, and so, whenever possible, to be altered by purposive action based on reason. This is, perhaps, the unacknowledged assumption underlying much current moral skepticism. The other attitude is conservative (though it includes a special form of radicalism); it holds that institutions are the results of centuries of human adaptation and adjustment, of relative success, because the failures disappear, and so institutions are embodiments of collective human wisdom. They are, therefore, to be respected and defended, to be tampered with slowly, and only as wisdom develops through further historical experience.

Institutional arrangements are, however, neither perfect nor entirely accidental. Institutions have functions; and in the course of history have developed more or less successful ways in which people may cooperate to resolve their difficulties. Conventional morals are basic to institutional functions, and are usually tested means for the attainment of important human ends. Men are obligated to support their children, in order that the children survive and the race or society continue. Conventional morals are indeed morals, and are very much better than no morals at all. But—and I

---

*By critical morality I mean a morality that results from the evaluation and criticism of conventional morality, and thus is more than social habit and existent morality. Ways of criticizing conventional morality and its consequences will be detailed in Chapter Five.

shall discuss this in some detail later—they are often not what they might be, and so can be criticized.

What we have, then, on the part of the moral skeptic, is a decision that existent morality is not morality at all; it is, since another name is needed for it, social mores, or conventions. Why? Perhaps because existent moralities are relative. Then true morality would be universal. Perhaps because we can sometimes think of arrangements that would work better or perfectly. Then true morality is beyond criticism. Perhaps because we cannot show that a moral rule in one society is better in itself than a moral rule about the same issue in another society. Then true morality can be confirmed by some test. So true morality must be universal, beyond criticism, and confirmed by test. That is a very traditional description of the characteristics of morality (confirmation, traditionally, would be by revelation or some other ultimate authority) and it makes the philosopher a skeptic, for he cannot find such a morality outside the tradition, and he refuses to settle for anything less.

Such a situation is intellectually intolerable. It has its humor, yet it ceases to be funny when it keeps so many good minds from moral discourse and deprives the sciences of man of their moral component. But I have booed the villain long enough; it is time for the hero to enter.

Moral discourse has human conduct as its subject; it is a universe of discourse composed by the contradictories "moral," "immoral," and includes categories derived from them. Immoral conduct is as much a part of the moral universe of discourse as the night is of the day. If there is no possibility of immorality, there is no morality, for freedom to choose is a necessary condition of morality, and the choice must be between good and evil, or between the morally better and the morally worse. Whenever a man is forced to do something, whether good or bad, he is not, in that situation, a moral agent. If I am thrown from a height onto someone below, I am not responsible. If I am threatened with death, my moral agency is minimized. When a man is deprived of moral agency, his behavior is neither moral nor immoral, nor is he responsible for his actions, as he is when he is a moral agent.

In general—specifics will come later—what are the social functions of morality? What does it do? These questions could be asked in the tradition, but they would not be important, or at least their answers would have no bearing on morality itself. What is right, is right, in the traditional view, and so it should be done, whatever its consequences. But *morals are made for men, not men for morals.* So the functions, the uses, the consequences of morality bear on the morality we choose, and provide its justification. Of course, men are by nature social, and so moral, for there cannot be human society without morals or, perhaps, morals without society. There can be insect societies without morals, but man has gained reason as he lost instinct, and his society does not always function blindly, but also by virtue of decision and morals. So morals are not made for man as clothes are, to cover his natural nakedness; morals are made for man as art is, fulfilling an aspect of human nature.

Morals function to increase the probability that men will attain their ends. Morals replace force by cooperative behavior, or minimize force and maximize cooperation. Morals also reduce the results of conditioning and habituation and increase rational choice and voluntary action. Since both force and conditioning minimize or eliminate responsibility, it is morals that make men responsible. When a given system or code of morals fails to function in these ways, or functions poorly, it is open to criticism, alteration, or replacement.

Let me explain this view, which is neither traditional nor scientistic.

CHAPTER FOUR

The Locus of Obligation

The distinction between person and status is important for the intellectual health of the sciences of man. In psychology, behaviorists have sometimes reduced statuses to persons (and persons to animals) as though all that were true of politicians could be learned from the human or subhuman animal. Some rat leader will perhaps one day be studied to test the maxims of Machiavelli. In sociology and political science, behavioralists and functionalists have sometimes reduced persons to statuses, as though people were only coordinates in a network of social lines, with no inner lives of their own. In ethics, the distinction is of great significance because quite different considerations are appropriate to persons and to statuses.

All persons in society occupy statuses, which are recognized positions with specifiable functions. Robinson Crusoe, alone on his island, was carpenter, fisherman, and cook, but those were personal functions, things he did to survive, not the functions of social position. In society, men enter and leave statuses, no matter how rigidly fixed the statuses are, being in turn husbands, fathers, widowers, and grandfathers, ceasing to be husbands when they become widowers, but not necessarily when they become fathers. What is vital to ethics is that statuses carry duties, not just functions and roles, and that to some extent the two are one. The principle that emerges is: values are of persons; obligations fall on statuses.

As persons, considered apart from all status, each of us lives in a world of advantage and disadvantage, and what is advantageous to one man may be disadvantageous to another, because our personalities and circumstances differ. It is fortunate for social life that this is so; if it were not, identical personalities in similar circumstances would compete more directly for the scarce goods of this world, making them even scarcer. As it is, if you want excitement and I want calm, we can go our separate ways.

Advantage, then, is personal and variable; it is what we like and what we want. To be sure, the statuses we occupy, like everything else that happens to us, mold and alter our persons, but it is as persons, not as statuses, that we like and want. Typical of the human condition, what we like is not always good for us, no matter how much we want it or how hard we try to get it. To know what we want we feel and respond, on the basis of antecedents, impulse, desire and taste, and objects and situations; to discover what is good for us we look to consequences. What we want is dependent on emotion; what is good for us on reflection. On the ground that we will be better off if we can want what is good for us, we call what benefits us "value" or "good," terms we approve more than "desire" or "advantage." And as we move to the good, we go from the subjective to the objective, from the purely personal to the interpersonal, because what we like and want may be irrelevant to the welfare of others, but what we value and find good will have to take the welfare of others into account. Reflection on consequences will include consequences for others.

More concretely, if I like and want to eat strawberries, and they are plentiful and easily picked by me, I do little or no harm to others if I eat them. If the demand for strawberries is greater than the supply, their price will be high in a market economy, and I must weigh my wants to decide whether I prefer to pay the price for the strawberries or save my money for a new shirt. If strawberries make me sick, or are so expensive I have to cut down on my children's milk to eat them, I become concerned with what is good for me, the consequences of eating strawberries and with what is moral, my duties to my children. The former is based on good or value—how much do I value health?—the latter on my duty as a father as well as my love for my children.

Value is in the realm of the person, but not in that of one person alone, except perhaps for that limiting case, Crusoe before he found Friday. Value is the result of reflection on appetite, impulse, and desire, using, ideally, all the resources of the means-ends continuum. The difference between value and good is not in their content, but in their connections to the psyche. I may not know that x is good, although it is, and I may not act to attain it. But either I know consciously what I value, or I act in such a way as to reveal it. A pervasive philosophical doctrine, that men naturally seek the good, has always been qualified by the comment that they may not know the good. That, after all, is how knowledge came to be thought virtue.

If I do know the good, or think I do, am I obligated to try to realize it? In Platonic ethics, where men naturally seek the good, I should have no such obligation, for what I do by nature, I must do, and I cannot be obligated to do what I must do, any more than I can be obligated to do what I can't do.* Those Greeks whose ethics were based on the good, could not, therefore, develop a theory of obligation in the modern sense. Since to seek the good, however, requires that one know the good, there is a kind of Greek obligation to be intelligent, to try to know.

Greek theory somewhat neglects both the Hebrew Right and genuine obligation in the social sense, which is a type of constraint, but it is paradigmatic for value theory. If I decide it is good for me to be healthy, although it means suppressing appetite, and I am convinced that exercise is a necessary condition of health, then I am in a sense obligated to exercise. To generalize, I am obligated to do what intelligence discovers to be means to the realization of a value. (And I am under a basic obligation to know what those means are, if I can.) But not, again, if I must seek the good because it is my nature to do so; only (denying Plato) if I may choose, knowing the good, to seek it or not. In other words, I only have obligations if I may violate them (although, of course, I shouldn't).

Since obligation can exist only where there is choice, there seems to be a question whether the choice, in the matter of values, is of means or ends. I think the answer is ends. Of course I can choose not to perform the means, but that only means choosing not to fulfill an obligation; it does not mean I do not

---

*In the full Platonic argument to know the good includes control and direction of the emotions by that knowledge. Then, of course, to know the good means to do the good. But surely this is a tautology.

have that obligation. It is by choosing the end, however, that I acquire the obligation, and I may choose or reject an end, but I do not choose whether or not to have the obligation that goes with it. Value theory reveals that the realm of the person is, ethically, a realm of hypothetical imperatives in the traditional sense. If I value health, I am obligated to exercise, or to do whatever else reason and knowledge show will yield health. This hypothetical imperative, this form of obligation demanded by either value or good, is still a refinement of the *search* for advantage, as value and good are refinements of advantage. Yet the refinement introduces obligation, for there is no obligation to seek one's advantage; man simply has a propensity to do so.

Perhaps the whole notion of axiological obligation, obligation based on value, is that seeking the good means both trying to discover it and trying to bring it about. Both are exercises of intelligence, although the latter requires action as well, and the injunction to lead the good life is an injunction to live intelligently. That is a refrain of Greek ethics. It has confused the central issue of morals, which is obligation, when it has been assumed that obligation is essentially in the realm of the person and his values. Plato and Aristotle, to be sure, found much of the fulfillment of man in the *polis,* and did not separate ethics from politics, but they treated the *polis* as an extension of man (for Plato it was the individual writ large), and morality as though it were no different from axiology. But it is. The moral, or deontological, is a separate, though complementary world, in which obligations cannot be predicated of persons, but of statuses, a distinction the Greeks did not make.

It may be useful to call the world of social obligation "morality," or "morals," in distinction from value, and to keep the word "ethics" for the whole which includes morals and values, for in the end they must be related to each other. There is little point in subscribing to a morality that violates all my values, all I think good. Social obligation may be called "duty," as opposed to personal obligation, which is in the realm of value. I create a personal obligation when, for example, I freely and voluntarily make a promise, which is a statement that I will regard myself as obligated to do something. Some promises are made as occupants of statuses, rather than persons, and then they are social obligations. If a businessman agrees to deliver goods at a specified date,

he has a social obligation to do so, backed by courts of law. A
promise is more than a prediction, for nonfulfillment of the promise is not just error in forecasting; I am responsible for keeping the
promise, and my failure is a failure of responsibility, not just of
knowledge of the future.

Human society makes duty and status correlative. When I
accept employment of a given kind I acquire the duties that go
with it. When I resign, if I may, I no longer have those duties. If I
marry, I have one set of duties; if I divorce, another. Throughout
life I acquire and lose duties, whoever or whatever I am as a
person. Of course, duties may be somewhat altered by the force or
weakness of the person occupying a status, but they are the duties
of the status that are altered, not the duties of the person, and it
may be that the next person to occupy that status will inherit the
altered duties. Fundamentally, though, we do not invent our
duties; we discover them.

Morality is necessary to society; it is everywhere a part of
the social fabric. Considerable acceptance of official, or conventional, morality is necessary for the continuance, efficiency, and
well-being of a society. If society's norms are not internalized by
its members and its obligations are not accepted, there will probably be a proportionate increase in the amount of force employed
to ensure that functions are performed and order maintained. Increase in the use of internal force is an indication of instability
and, in the end, may contribute to the increase of instability,
rather than its eradication.

Fundamental to occupation of status is membership in a
group which has statuses in it; and membership in the group is
itself a status, like being a citizen of France. First, logically,
among memberships is that in a society, however it is conceived,
as nation, tribe, or kingdom. After that, there is membership in
institutions and systems, like business and the kinship system.
Finally, there is membership in smaller groups, like this business
firm, which employs me, and this family in which I am husband,
son, father. My statuses are my membership and positions in those
groups and my social obligations, or duties, are in general the
functions of my statuses. Normally, I am not forced to perform
those functions—although there may be constant external reinforcement of my desire to do so, including threats—because I accept them as obligatory, even if I have some qualifications about

them. And it is not I, as a person, on whom these obligations fall, but anyone who occupies the statuses.

Social obligation is an asymmetrical relation between a group and its members. People have certain duties by virtue of membership in a group, but the group does not have the same duties to its members. A group is not a mob or crowd, like shoppers in department stores. A group, like an institution, which is one kind of group, is an organization of men for one or more purposes. Shoppers in department stores have purposes but no organization. Their purposes are individual, even when they are the same, in that shoppers are, to a considerable extent, competing with each other. Competition, of course, may be a form of cooperation, but only in a larger context of shared purposes and organization to attain them. An army, on the other hand, has purposes, shared in some way by its members, and organization as well. Organization is necessary because the purposes of a group are realizable only by the organized behavior of its members or of a number of them.

Smith, who is enlisted in the army, owes his superior officer certain things. He ought, for example to obey military commands. But he does not have that obligation by virtue of the fact that Brown and not Jones is his superior officer. He would have the obligations if Jones were his superior. Equally, he would not have any obligation of that sort if he were not in the army, and so not a military subordinate. Obligation is owed by virtue of membership in a group and falls on one as member and in his position in the group, both being statuses. Obligation is universal insofar as it holds for all who have membership or occupy a certain position in a group. Thus, the obligations of President of the United States are obligations not merely of Mr. Polk or Mr. Fillmore, but of all who hold the position.

At this point we can formulate two principles, which define obligation. The first is a general principle of obligation: if A is a member of group B then he is obligated to do x under conditions y. The second increases the intension, and usually decreases the extension, by specifying status beyond that of mere membership: if A holds position C in group B, then he is obligated to do r under conditions s, in addition to his obligations sheerly as member. How can we discover what in fact are the obligations of A and the conditions under which they exist, since they are to be discovered,

not invented? By examining the results of fulfillment and nonfulfillment of what, hypothetically, we think those obligations to be;
results, that is, in the sense of behavior toward A by the group, in
its official capacity, or on the part of other members, as members,
in consequence of his action.

Here we see a second sense of obligation, entirely compatible
with the first. Obligation is an expectation of determinate behavior, fostered by the rules, implicit and explicit, of the group. In
the simplest case, if A is rewarded for fulfillment of what we
thought to be his obligation under specified conditions, we conclude that we were probably right. Just so, if he is punished for
nonfulfillment. In practical affairs, every nuance of reward and
punishment exists and we may, as in any other matters of fact, be
misled by incorrect observation or misinterpretation of what we
experience.

The locus of obligation, then, is the group, and obligations
themselves (social obligations, or duties) are functions of the status
of membership, and of special statuses within the organization of
the group. This is conventional morality; it exists in the same way
groups and statuses and functions exist; it is the moral aspect of
the factual, the "ought" in the "is." Conventional morality is
made up of obligations discoverable in the workings of society. It
performs its own vital functions of minimizing the use of force
and maximizing cooperation when most members of society expect obligations to be fulfilled, by others and themselves. This set
of expectations is a psychological constraint, which can be stated
as the categorical imperative of conventional morality: Accept in
your person the obligations of your statuses.

Yet even if all I have argued is true, there remain the questions of justification and criticism. I do not believe that there is a
different question: how can we construct another, separate, uncrit-
icizable morality, universal and absolute? A better morality than
any given conventional morality is the result of criticizing conventional morality, and so constructing a reflective or critical morality, not an entirely different one. If we created an entirely different morality *ab initio,* it would be properly subject to many of
the strictures of the moral skeptic, strictures which are beside the
point when we deal with existent and critical morality. It would
also, I think, be based on an old error about the nature of moral

philosophy: that it is a construction of human reason dealing with questions of how men ought to behave, and necessarily excluding all concern with how men do behave (for that is "anthropology," not ethics).

The analogy of this mistaken idea of moral philosophy is to logic, which deals with forms of valid inference, and excludes the actual inferences men make, as well as the psychology of thought. The analogy has kept moral philosophy from the heat and grime of practice and politics, where it belongs, and made it so pure that a great philosopher could insist that no man ever tell the most trivial lie, even to save life. Moral philosophy of this sort supports the notion that men are made for morals, not morals for men; it makes the right all and the good nothing. But logic can be genuinely a priori, whatever its origins, and properly spurn actual thought, unless it wants to show its structure. Moral philosophy, however, can no more be a priori than aesthetics.

Moral philosophy is not to be conceived as having its own subject matter, as mathematics has; it has rather its own way of treating a subject matter with which other disciplines are concerned in other ways. The analogy is not to logic; it is rather to the *philosophy* of science, which is not itself science, but which uses science as subject; or the *philosophy* of art, or society, or religion. The special way in which philosophy deals with these matters is analytic, critical, and evaluative.

But, we may be asked, on what basis can moral philosophy criticize or evaluate? In answer, let us first broaden the question. On what basis can the philosophy of science or of art criticize or evaluate? And do they? Or should they? The questions answer themselves.

Although the subject matter of the philosophy of science is science, the subject matter of science is nature. The subject matter of art is not art but experience; nor is the subject of morals morals, but conduct. Art, science, and morals, which are both types and products of human behavior, are themselves subjects for the historian, the sociologist, the critic, and the philosopher. There is a history of art and a sociology of art, but neither is art itself. The philosopher's material will come in part from the historian and the sociologist, but his conclusions, which may be material for their study, are directly related to the work of the critic, as the conclusions of the scientist are related to the work of the technician. Science is applied to yield technology; philosophy is applied to yield criticism; it provides the grounds, the criteria, of criticism. And as the critic may not only criticize but propose, so the moral critic may also be a moralist.

Moral philosophy should be based on knowledge of conventional morals and their historical and institutional context, as philosophy of science is based on knowledge of science and the procedures of scientists. Like philosophy of art or science, it should start with description, go on to analysis, and continue to criticism and evaluation of existing valuations.

The grounds of criticism are of the utmost importance; without them we have no way of arriving at a critical morality, and are trapped in the belief that whatever is, is right, or we oppose the passion of intuition and emotion, themselves conditioned by the rhetoric of conventional morality, to the reality of conventional morality. In this second case, current existent morality may be attacked either from the standpoint of a presumably better past or from that of an antagonistic ethical philosophy which could lead to a presumably better future. Little sober criticism comes in these ways, especially when the ethical philosophy chosen is essentially a theory of value, not of obligation. The instinct is right, nonetheless, that seeks to judge obligation by standards of value which are, in the end, its justification.

We are, of course, born into a society and a family, and enter our early statuses unthinkingly. But our membership, statuses, and obligations are not just there, like the trees of the forest. However irrational human society is, its organization yet bears some marks of purpose. And however automatically men enter and leave groups, they may ask that the groups, and their own places in them, be justified.

The existence of a group or institution is justified, I think, by four conditions: (1) that it acts to attain the purposes of its members; (2) that the members cannot attain those purposes, or cannot attain them as well, by individual action; (3) that there is no other group to which the members could as readily belong which attains the same purposes better; (4) that even if the members could do as well alone, the cost (in time, energy, money, or other values) would be too great. As an instance of the logic underlying the formation of a new group: in a society in which education takes place entirely in the home, with parents teaching their own children, too much may be learned by the society to continue in this way, or greater vocational activity may make it harder for parents to give as much time to their children as they used to. An obvious solution is for several parents to pay someone to teach all their children.

Almost immediately there are difficulties. If the number of children is great, there should be more than one teacher. No one's home will be large enough to house the school. If a schoolhouse is acquired, it must be cleaned and heated. If there are several teachers, there must be a structure of authority and administration. There must be a levy of some sort on the parents, so the costs are met. There should be an organization of parents to make decisions on these matters, and on any others, such as whether parents should pay in proportion to the number of children they have, the size of their incomes, or the amount of work they do to help out with the school.

The decisions made by the parents constitute a set of means to yield the ends they share. The existence of the school is justified if it meets the criteria set out above, and the same criteria justify membership of the parents in the group. What becomes apparent at this point is that *the means decided upon are identical with the obligations of the members.* There is no other rationale for obligation that I can see, and no other justification. At the same time, the possibility of criticism appears: if the means are carried out, will that yield the group ends the members want and share? If we think not, then criticism of the means employed by the group is also, because of their identity, criticism of the obligations of its members. This is the birth of moral criticism.

I shall devote the next chapter to moral criticism and critical morality. This one would be incomplete without some comment on responsibility to round out the analysis of obligation.

Moral agency and responsibility are inextricable. If one is a moral agent, he is responsible for his actions. This is accepted not only by moral philosophers but by moral skeptics, for whom denial of responsibility is sometimes the chief argument against the possibility of morals. But "responsibility" is used in many ways in moral theory, and often its meanings conflict. So if a man acts under compulsion, he is said not to be responsible for his act. Who is? Presumably whoever made him act as he did, if there are such persons; and there may not be, for compulsion can be internal. Responsibility in this sense follows from uncoerced decision and action. But a common expression states that government is, or ought to be, responsible to its citizenry. That seems a different use of "responsibility," making it a relation between two parties. It is possible, of course, to say that our first use, the uncoerced act, is that of moral responsibility and the second is not. But the demand that government be responsible to its citizenry is surely more than political. Politically, it means that the conduct of government should not only be judged by its subjects, but that their judgment should be effective, their approval or disapproval decisive for the future. That much might be asked in the name of efficiency. But more underlies it.

Responsibility has to do with response, and a response is an answer. When a man does something of his own volition, he is answerable for it, he must respond when asked to justify it, he is accountable. When he is made to do something, it is important to affix responsibility for his action, and so discover who is answerable, if anyone is. The Kafkaesque quality of much bureaucracy is that things are done but no one is answerable for them. When we ask that government be responsible to its citizenry, we want it to be answerable, to justify its actions in virtue of the values of its people and the ends they share as citizens. Responsibility, it will emerge, is essentially the same whether it be predicated of a person or a government.

Here we reach the heart of the moral enterprise. The human dialogue is one of questions and answers, and the moral dialogue is one of questions and answers about conduct. If we are not to be alone, or alienated, if we are to escape solitary confinement within the human breast, we must be bound to each other, as we are by moral bonds, and we must be answerable to each other. Responsibility is a way of finding our course by having to justify our action.

But morality is not only there, in man's world, to be discovered by the discerning eye, criticized, and remade. It is itself, once discovered, answerable to the question, "Is it good?" So often we feel in bondage to morality, held back from our desires by its chains. Surely we want to pad the chains, keep the bite from our wrists, but we are entitled to still more, to ask whether we want them at all. In more traditional philosophies this may not be a real question. "Ought we to be moral?", the question that has been asked, dissolves when it is shown that whatever we "ought" to do is by definition moral. But "Is it good to be moral?" is another question, partly answered by what I have said about dialogue and solitude.

We can put the question a little differently when we realize that the only alternative to being moral agents is solitude on an island or in the grave. For then we know that the value of living and of living with others makes it good to be moral, in the sense of being within morality, of having moral agency. And the question we can ask is how much moral agency we want for each of us. Some one, of course, must accept a great deal of moral agency if others accept little or none.

Morality involves responsibility, as it involves freedom. Freedom is necessary for morality, and morality is necessary for responsibility. So responsibility, too, requires freedom. Responsibility, though, which means being answerable, is being answerable to a questioner. In a way, we are answerable to anyone who questions us, and demands that we justify our conduct. Responsibility in that sense is justifiability, accounting for our conduct to the world in the terms that justify it. But responsibility is also to those who are entitled to question. Thus we are responsible to the groups in which we are members, and to the other members of those groups. This kind of responsibility is fundamental, for those are the groups whose terms are our terms.

A Quaker, for example, is more responsible to Quakers for his conduct with respect to war than he is to Roman Catholics. So long as he is a member of the group, Quakers, he must justify his actions by appeal to Quaker principles. His justification to the world is based on those principles, which lead to the end he shares with other Quakers, and the means to attain them. If responsibility to the Quakers conflicts with the society within which Quakers exist, and of which he is a member, then he puts the Quaker morality first, and is a special case in his society, or he puts the society first, and is a special case among Quakers.

Dialogue of this sort is also implicit. If we say a man is

responsible, we mean he fulfills his obligations and so *could* answer for his actions if questioned. It is the possibility of questions and the ability to justify conduct in answer that makes up responsibility. It follows that the potential question and the ability to respond keeps us responsible; the legitimate questioner is one to whom we are responsible. An absolute ruler might eliminate all questioners but himself. That does not end his own moral agency, which is dependent on freedom and power, but it minimizes the possibility of moral conduct. The absolute ruler's accountability to himself is still within a social context and has to do with the consequences of his conduct for others, but it may leave his conduct somewhat capricious. The internal questioner mirrors, and may replace, the outer questioners. Sometimes the internal questioner refines the questions that might be asked from the outside, and the interrogation approaches the ideal. Sometimes the internal questioner is stilled or rationalizes duty to conform to self-advantage.

The internal questioner (conscience?) is less likely to be arbitrary or capricious when there are external questioners as well, whose judgment of the ruler's responses may alter his future conduct. This group is thus more secure if its rulers are responsible to it, and if it has the power—which requires freedom as a condition—to assure its effect. The ruler is usually more moral then in his conduct, but no more or less a moral agent because his freedom of choice assures his moral agency whether his responsibility is to himself alone or to others. Freedom and power are conditions of moral agency; responsibility is a condition of moral conduct; responsibility to others, especially to the group as a whole, is a safeguard of moral conduct.

This safeguard is the neglected problem, it seems to me, of Dostoevski's "Grand Inquisitor," of the "escape from freedom," of the crushing burden of individual responsibility, because the psychic price of moral agency is so great that many people are pleased if others pay the price and make the decisions. The answer to the question of responsibility to whom has been given differently in different societies, and we are all born into societies which have structured their answers into institutions. But the question must always be asked again, because it is fundamental to the conditions of human life.

Morality as a web of obligation—we dare not call it a system because of its many inconsistencies—should not be confused with that pseudomorality which is a web of commands. To demand morality and moral agency fully is necessarily to demand considerable freedom to discover obligation, to fulfill it or deliberately not fulfill it, and to criticize and change it. And that underlies what we want of government, including our insistence that government be responsible to its citizens. For if government is not responsible, citizens do not have control of the conditions for their own freedom. One of the greatest political delusions is the belief that we can exchange political liberties—those that keep government responsible to us—for benefits like security, because we are then insecure in our security; it can be taken from us by another's will.

We do not have a real choice between all men being moral agents or no men being moral agents, for some men must be moral agents fully and some less fully. The question is whether all men— or most—are to be moral agents fully, or only some small number, who rule them. There must be moral agency because there must be morals. The question is also one of human freedom under government: who rules, how responsible the rulers are, and how much freedom the rulers and the ruled have. So the basic question about morals—which is a matter of value—is also the basic question about politics. We have to have both morals and politics, and our fundamental decision in each case is about moral agency. That decision implies a number of things about government and limits its forms, for only some forms will be consistent with our decision about morals. Again, the question is about function: the structural forms that best yield the functions we want are matters of secondary decision; although they may have been decided implicitly by history, they can be re-decided explicitly by reason. Nature may be Darwinian, in that structure precedes function, but because human 'decision enters, society is Lamarckian, in that function precedes structure; rationally, we can create social structures that perform the functions we desire.

Although "responsibility" seemed at the start of this comment to have two distinct meanings, (1) uncoerced decision and action, and (2) an interaction of government and its citizens, the two are now clearly related: (2) is a condition of (1) when we choose to allow all people a maximization of uncoerced decision and action. For to carry out that action requires a government that permits and supports it, and so a government responsible to the people if permission and support are to continue.

As for the choice itself, that all men are to be fully moral agents, it is no more than deciding that we do not want men to be less than they naturally are. Living in total isolation is unnatural for a social creature, being stopped from thinking is unnatural for a rational creature, and not being a moral agent is unnatural for a moral creature. Man is naturally moral because he is naturally social. He is not just one of the social animals; he is the only social animal in any full sense. Some animals are gregarious, and some live in cooperation enforced by instinct, but any honest description of society ("human" society only when we want to emphasize a continuity with other animals) must grant eacn society its own culture, with an adaptation and adjustment based, at least in part, on reason, and with a moral framework. To want man to be a moral agent is no more than to want man to be man. And that, too, is the reason for making a political choice that allows and supports freedom, for the freedom of each is a necessary condition for the moral agency of all. Moral agency is eroded by many things, and no nation is blessed with a citizenry of full moral agents, but the scale runs from democratic nations to totalitarian nations.

The idea of responsibility can be clarified by the description of obligation. A is expected to do x, we said, under conditions y, when A is a member of group B. But A is not obligated *to* group B; he is obligated by virtue of being a member of B. Put differently, A is responsible to B to fulfill obligations that derive from his membership (and statuses) in B.* Obligation, as I stated, is an asymmetrical relation between members and a group. Responsibility, under conditions that maximize moral agency (i.e., under conditions of genuine obligation, not just command), is symmetrical. The member is responsible to his group in that his acts are judged effectively, so that group approval or disapproval makes a difference in practice; just so with the group's responsibility to its

---

*A is obligated to do x because he is a member of B. If x is "feeding one's children," then he is obligated *to* his children, to feed them. But A is answerable, or responsible, to B for feeding his children; he is not answerable to the children.

members. Thus "responsibility" has the same meaning when we are responsible for our acts and government is responsible to the governed.

The group is the locus of social obligation, and we are properly responsible to it for our moral acts. Obligations of membership are universal to members, to be sure, but relative to the group. All Quakers are under equal obligation not to go to war, but other citizens may not have such an obligation. So, too, with obligations falling on statuses within the group. Professional soldiers have acquired special obligations about war. From this standpoint, how can we deal with traditional moral disputes about, for example, universality and relativity?

Let us look at both the question of the hypothetical or categorical nature of obligation and that of the universality or relativity of morals. The first question is often prejudiced by a feeling that the idea of morality as a set of hypothetical moral imperatives (if A, then one ought to do B) is spurious, and that obligation is categorical (one ought to do B—without any qualification) or it is not genuinely obligation at all. Curiously, some people who feel that way are content to interpret all scientific law as hypothetical, and so implicitly accept more qualification of statements in physics than they would of statements in morals. Yet whether we find obligations to be hypothetical or categorical is a matter of logical convention. I have stated the nature of obligation hypothetically: "*If* A is a member of group B . . ." And one may state any generalization hypothetically: "All men are mortal," a categorical, becomes "For all values of x, if x is a man, then x is mortal." But if we want to start with a statement of existence, the very same generalization can be categorical: "There are men. Everything that is a man must be mortal." So, too, with obligation: "There are members of group B. Every member of group B has the obligation . . ." We are talking of existent obligation, to be sure, but we can be equally hypothetical or categorical about critical obligation.

Kant's famous categorical imperative can be distinguished from hypothetical imperatives if the latter have the form: "If you want x, you should do y"; and the former can be stated, as Kant stated it: "So act that . . ."* But to whom is the categorical addressed? To men, of course, all men at all times and places, without qualifying conditions. And that presumably makes it categorical. Yet one can, if he likes, use for Kant's categorical imperative the same logical convention customarily applied to empirical generalizations: "For all values of x, if x is a man, x is obligated so to act that . . ." Now the same imperative is hypothetical. Two distinctions can still be made between the categorical imperative as Kant understood it, and my analysis of the obligations of men by virtue of membership in groups. Kant's imperative is general, and all particular imperatives can be derived from it; Kant's imperative is unqualified by time, place, and circumstance. On the first count, the "categorical" imperative is too general to have real content, as its critics have noted. On both counts, its virtue does not consist in its categoricalness, but in its universality.

So the issue of categorical or hypothetical imperatives can be treated as a matter of logical convention, except insofar as the issue becomes that of the universality or relativity of morals. And that, too, is an inflated problem. The idea of a universal morality is most attractive, to be sure, and normally includes the belief that such a morality is certain. Yet whenever a universal and certain morality has been proclaimed, it has soon been hedged with so many qualifications that it is no more useful than a relative morality, and perhaps no different. That is not an easily accepted idea. The ferocity with which an absolutist in morals often attacks the idea of moral relativity is an indication of the distance he feels from it; and the disdain with which he views relativity reveals his belief that it cannot do the job required of morals. Objectors to relativity in morals cite the impossibility of condemning Nazism and other barbarisms unless there is an absolute base for ethics. At the least, they want acceptance of natural law.

The great attraction of natural law theory is that it provides an alternative, or rational complement, to belief in the will of God as the arbiter of morals. If offers a universal and timeless morality

---

*Kant distinguished sharply between his categorical imperative, so act that you would wish the principle of your action to be a universal law, and all hypothetical imperatives. The former was universal and unqualified; the latter were neither. Kant clung thus to the traditional belief that genuine morality was absolute and universally binding.

which all can discover. If there is not included in it a special doctrine of revealed law with which it may not conflict, natural law is the product of right reason. It is the set of moral beliefs all rational men would accept on the twin bases of the nature of man and the human condition. "Natural" law is opposed to "social" law because natural law is not relative to any culture, and it underlies all societies, as nature does.

Yet what one decides natural law is depends on one's view of human nature and the human condition. So advocates of natural law may be political conservatives,* as so many of them are today, Thomistic liberals, or political radicals. Natural law was appealed to by the conservative Hobbes, the liberal Locke, and French revolutionaries. Apart from this difficulty, which alone should be sufficient to cool the ardor of many for natural law, there is the problem of all universal morals: it has to be applied to different cultures and special situations, and when it is it yields different moral rules for all of them. This may not seem an insuperable problem; juridical law, too, must consider the circumstances in each case to which it is applied. But it takes away almost any benefit of accepting natural law when we ask whether natural law has any virtue that relative morality has not. That is a reasonable and important question if we believe morals are made for men, not men for morals.

As we apply universal morals to different times and places, the disparity in moral rules for various circumstances may be so great that there is little value in the original universality. Jacques Maritain, who is an absolutist in morals, believing in natural law and divine law, thinks that though there could be no excuse for the Inquisition in our time, there might have been justification for it when it actually flourished. Casuistry is a necessary corollary of universality, when one starts from absolute, not relative morality, and casuistry may suggest a different rule for every situation.

When we do start with relative morality, uncriticized and unrefined, and try to extend it to ever-larger groupings, we often end with approximately the same obligations that result from absolute morality. We discover what two groups have in common, or what would not conflict with their individual moral schemes, or

*I have in mind Leo Strauss and his followers, as well as some members of the New Conservativism.

what would be an acceptable compromise. Then, as we keep extending morality, we move toward something like the obligation the absolute moralist started with. He, in turn, taking into consideration the realities of individual and group circumstances, is likely to end where the relative moralist began.

Almost any absolutist in the West, religious or secular, starting with the universal commandment "Thou shalt not kill," qualifies it at once by assuming that only other men are intended. Even if he becomes a vegetarian because he will not exclude animals, he draws an artificial line at vegetables, which die when picked. Then reflection qualifies the command further by allowing us to kill men in self-defense (why should others be allowed to kill us?) and before long the realities of the national state make it moral to kill external enemies in war and fellow-nationals who commit treason. The relativist, if he started with separate moral codes that allow killing men for different offenses, from adultery among the Eskimo to witchcraft among fifteenth-century Europeans, and sought a common principle underlying all the kinds of official killing and official injunctions against killing, might arrive at "Thou shalt not kill, except officially, or with the sanction of a moral code." And that is what the absolutist belief amounts to.

Neither the absolutist nor the relativist position has the virtue of the critical position here maintained, in which the existent morality of each group is first rendered conscious (discovered), and then criticized and refined, thus transforming it into reflective or critical morality, before seeking to accommodate it to superordinate or allied groups, whose morality has been similarly transformed. And only critical morality has the advantages of being based on empirical study of the needs and conditions of men and society, and of using the full range of intelligence to refine and extend morals. Understanding and making morality in this sense is a vast and difficult enterprise, for which I am, at most, writing a program.

CHAPTER FIVE

Critical Morality

Critical morality originates in the criticism of existent morality. When we find what is wrong with existent morality, we may propose social obligations (critical morality) that would, presumably, do better. The temporary end of the process is the substitution of critical obligation for conventional obligation; when that happens, the critical obligation becomes a conventional one, and the process of criticism and substitution starts again. Conversion of critical morality into existent morality is either an implicit decision, due to changes in attitudes, beliefs, and expectations which come with time and historical change or an explicit decision, a consequence of group deliberation. In the latter case, the conversion occurs in law or in the overt decision of those with authority in a group. Law can, for example, end polygamy and enforce monogamy; a father and mother can alter the obligations of their children.

Criticism of conventional morality is not an a priori matter of comparing what exists with what, supposedly, should exist. It is a practical and empirical matter of the relations of obligations to the ends they are presumed to serve and to the other consequences they yield. What are the criteria by which we can judge obligations poor, inadequate or wrong? There are a number of them and more than one may have to be used in any case. Without pretending to exhaust those criteria, I shall list twelve, noting they are not entirely separate.

1. The obligations of members should, when fulfilled, yield group ends.

2. Obligations within a group should be consistent.

3. Obligations to different groups should not conflict with each other.

4. The process of decision-making should be rational and effective.

5. Especially when a group is part of a larger group, some obligations should have precedence over others.

6, Obligations should be suited to the functional prerequisites of society.

7. Obligations should support the ethos of a culture, unless it is decided to alter that ethos.

8. Each person should accept the obligation to conduct himself privately so he can fulfill his social obligations.

9. No person should accept obligations (where he has a choice) that he cannot fulfill.

10. The shared ends of a group should realize the values of its members.

11. Obligations to mankind should be considered in relation to group obligation.

12. As circumstances change so that existent obligations no longer yield group ends, the obligations should be changed so that they do.

It is utopian, of course, to think that all these criteria could ever be realized, yet they are the source of genuine moral criticism. I shall consider them in this chapter, although not in the above order, along with other matters relevant to them. The twelfth criterion, though, will only be mentioned, for it brings special difficulties, which will be treated at length in the following chapter. I shall start here with a word about the relations of law and morality.

Existent morality is the only morality most people know. In its complex web, men find their obligations and law its work. Whatever the proper task of legislation is, the law goes so far as to protect the feelings of the majority by proscribing conduct that might affront its moral sensibilities or show a bad example to its young. What else are laws that close shops or prohibit the sale of liquor on Sundays? Law in nations like England and the United States is not supposed to protect the moral beliefs of any one religion, but since the majority subscribes to one religion, or similar ones, the law enforces monogamy.

In its more direct dealings with morality, law adds specified and surer punishment as a price for violating obligations, and it may even formulate obligations that have not yet been discovered or agreed on by many people. It does so in the relations of labor and management, for example, or in the regulation of business practices. On the other hand, law may merely reinforce obligations that are quite generally understood, but too often violated or neglected. By making an obligation legal, legislation renders it explicit and subject to thought and due process, and so more readily changeable; indeed, by selecting among, and articulating obligations, law is an implicit criticism of obligations. And, paradoxically, law makes obligation both more stable and more corrigible.

Law and morality by no means always complement each other. Some of the greatest crises of civilization result from the decision of a ruling class to oppose the conventional morals of a nation by making them illegal, or by making violation of them mandatory. That is the practice of the Hitlers and Stalins of this world, but in some degree also the practice of imperial powers in the treatment of colonies, and of semi-permanent majorities (of religion, race, and tribal membership, for example) in the treatment of minorities. And the relation of law to existent morality can be a question for critical morality. But these are problems to consider in another place; what is important here is that when law and morality coincide, the rationale of the obligation is initially the same, although obligation to obey the law, which has its own grounds, is a reinforcement of each specific obligation that enters law.

The rationale of law and morals is, briefly, that in order to attain shared ends, a set of means is agreed on within a group, and these become the obligations of members. Only in rudimentary groups, or at special times in others, are the means such that all members are expected to carry them out equally. Usually, members occupy different statuses, to which different means are appropriate. Coordination of all the activities which constitute means are, presumably, what makes the ends possible of attainment. Criticism of existent morality thus becomes more complex, for it is not just the actions expected of all members, but those of each status, plus the organization of those actions, that must be judged as appropriate or inappropriate means to the group's ends.

It is astonishingly hard to know whether our social obligations yield our shared ends. Even a comparatively rational organization like an American college may not, for all its struggles, educate its students. The words we use for our ends are usually general enough to be vague, like "security" or "justice," and "education" is no better. Do we mean to distinguish it from skill and training? To know whether our conduct as educators is effective, we must first be clear about the effects we want. Moral criticism should start with a strenuous effort to get such ideas clear, and only then go on to ask whether prescribed conduct does what it is supposed to do. When it does not, the more we internalize our obligations, and the more we do as we are expected to, the worse the effect. An accident often occurs: the man who fails to do what is prescribed may do what is needed. The class may teach itself when the teacher does not mislead it, or drill originality out of his students; education may take place in the moments when the teacher ruminates, or is silent.

Not to be minimized is the difficulty of finding means that yield an approximation of security, justice, or education. When existent obligation turns out not to be means to the cherished end, what obligation would be? A knowledge of cause and effect is indispensable, but how far can we generalize in dealing with people? What would educate me may stifle you. Yet how much can we allow individual differences to determine curricula and pedagogy when we try to educate all who are educable? And to what extent should teacher-student relationships be fixed in a pattern of obligation, since all teachers and students are different; to what extent should the relationship be based on individual judgment when institutional arrangements must be protected?

Real moral problems are exacerbated by a constant conflict of duty within any group. The teacher has obligations to the school that employs him, to the teaching profession, to the scholarly profession (physicists, economists, etc.) of which he is a member, to his students, and perhaps to the state or the private donors that support his school. Lack of conflict would be miraculous. Within a single family, a woman is often torn between the duties of a wife and those of a mother. And in larger organizations one has numerous statuses, each with its own obligations. Resolution of the dissonances and outright contradictions that emerge depends on clarity about the ends the organization is presumed to serve and the way statuses should be related to serve those ends. When the college teacher loses sight of education because of all the minor ends he sees too closely—pleasing the administration, keeping trustees content, giving students pleasure in his perform- ances, becoming well known in his professional association—he has lost his essential function, which is the basis for all the others. Yet to perform that function, which is his obligation as teacher, all his statuses and other functions within his school require coordina- tion. He is at once classroom teacher, student adviser, member of faculty committees, scholar or scientist, and so on. And he is all these in the interest of education, including his own lifelong edu- cation. His major function should be supported, not thwarted, by his subsidiary functions, and his statuses should mesh, not conflict. Yet that is rare.

Agreement within a group on the obligatory activities of its members is an agreement into which we are born, unless the group is new. Only on occasion do we make such agreements deliber- ately; they are normally part of inherited tradition. But they were made, usually slowly and over considerable time, and they need adjustment—sometimes, in crisis, rapid change—and enforcement. In one way or another, every group must be able to adjust and adapt, or it may perish.

Two of the conditions, then, for the continuing existence of any group are a process of arriving at group decision and a way of administering such decision. Neither of these need be rigidly fixed, nor must they remain the same, but without them a group cannot function; it loses all purpose. This is just a more detailed way of saying that since every group must be governed, it must have a government. Even if all members of a group participate equally in decision and administration, the group has government, for gov- ernment is defined by its function, not by its structure, whose variations in detail have been enormous through history.

Anarchists like Proudhon, Bakunin, and Kropotkin, who were utopians, but by no means naive, never succeeded in offering a refutation of government conceived realistically, in this fashion. They defined government in terms of what they took to be its essence: an ultimate use of force. But if it is true that all govern- ments of nations (and that is the only kind of government they were concerned with) have in fact rested on force, then that state- ment is either a generalization about the past that need not hold true for the future, or it articulates a necessity in governing large groups of men—because, for example, statistical deviation from the norm is predictable of all large groups and it requires force or its threat to protect the group from the deviant. But to define national rule as a reliance on force is by no means adequate for what, in extension, have regularly been named governments.

To call for a society in which coercion does not ultimately draw its strength from force, is very different from asking for a society without government. Indeed, it is not even to ask for a society in which all behavior would be uncoerced. Coercion would exist only in its milder forms of public and individual pressure in anarchist society, but it would exist. (One wonders whether there would also be vigilantism.) And all the talk of voluntary cooperation cannot mask the need for group, as distinguished from individual, decision. Even when such decision is made *by* an individual it is *for* a group. The most extreme form of individualist utopia would be a society in which the administration of group decision was entirely by obligation, fully felt and acted out. But how would that utopia criticize obligation, and how would it change?

The Marxian belief that the state will in time "wither away," is based as fully as any other anarchist doctrine—for it is one—on the conversion of a historical generalization into a definition. This might be called definition by hypothesis; it blurs the extension of the term defined. That the state is the executive committee of the ruling class, as Marxists maintain, is a factual generalization, or hypothesis, true or false, masquerading as a definition. The actual detail of the "state," bureaucracy, judiciary, army, etc., are structural elements of government varying in importance due to circumstance. Of course, the elements themselves vary somewhat, too, and have varied throughout history: professional army, volunteer army, conscript army, for example. But to predict—rightly or wrongly— that such elements of the state as armies and constabularies will one day disappear, is not to predict that governments will disappear. To make these seem one and the same prediction is a trick accomplished by substituting the contingent for the essential. Decision and administration are necessary to the group; and the people who decide and administer are the contingent personnel of government.

Merely to accept what is may be a necessity for some, but it is an implicit decision on the part of those who could do otherwise: despotisms, for example, may not interfere with family life, but they could; implicitly they may decide not to. National government, which has the power to do much that it does not do, is logically secondary: it may follow and administer what has already been decided, explicitly or implicitly, by the groups that make up the nation, it may interpret and alter their decisions, or it may oppose them. The decisions of most governments usually follow on the "decisions" of society, rather than precede them. Yet in both cases, that of nations and that of lesser groups, the basic subject matter of decisions, being means for the attainment of group ends or functions for the continuing realization of group purposes, are obligations, and are best implemented by their acceptance as obligatory, and the feeling of obligation. The quality of felt obligation is more than intellectual agreement; it involves conscience, emotions of solidarity that go with cooperation, and response to the expectations of others and to the behavior that follows from fulfilling or not fulfilling those expectations.

Feelings of obligation can be engendered even when one is wrong about what is obligatory, especially when one is surrounded by people wrong in the same way. Often this results in grotesque behavior. We see that behavior clearly in immigrants to a foreign land, displaced persons, and those who move rapidly from one rank of society to another, all those indeed who confront a set of obligations to which they have not been reared. A simple analogy is the confusion of manners when people of different cultures or of the same culture but different social ranks are together. No further evidence is necessary—although it can be found—that obligations exist whether or not they are felt and that there are feelings of obligation when in fact those obligations do not exist.

There are some, of course, who have identified all obligation with felt obligation. The emotive theory of morals does so, although its emphasis has been on the good, not the right, on advantage and value, not obligation and duty. The same emotive point can be made of both the good and the right, however: their meaning is an emotional response and we use statements that something is good or right to arouse such responses in others.

Basic to later emotive theories is a statement in Ogden and Richards' *The Meaning of Meaning:* *

> [The] peculiar ethical use of "good" is, we suggest, a purely emotive use. When so used the word stands for nothing whatever, and has no symbolic function . . . it serves only as an emotive sign expressing our attitude to *this,* and perhaps evoking similar attitudes in other persons, or inciting them to actions of one kind or another.

The emotive theory is the sort of idea that results from treating ethics as personal and interpersonal, but disconnected from society and politics. It is 'a form of reductionism. It does not stop at an analysis of the feelings that are aroused by ethical beliefs (which would be most useful), but identifies the very meaning of those beliefs with the feelings that accompany them.

The reductionism in Ogden and Richards' statement is what occurs when we translate sentence A into sentence B in such a way that the meaning of A is reduced in B. If I say "The United States is a sovereign nation" and am asked what that means, I may reply "The United States has the legitimate power to levy taxes." The second sentence reduces the meaning of the first, because "sovereign" includes more than taxation; it even includes the right to declare war. Just so, the statement "This is good" which means among other things that reflection shows "this" to have consequences we think desirable is reduced by Ogden and Richards to "an emotive sign expressing our attitude to *this.*" What is left out is the meaning of "This is good" which, supposedly, "stands for nothing whatever." What is substituted for the meaning of the statement is the emotion that may or may not accompany the statement. And that renders absurd a common and important type of behavior. Men are frequently engaged in discussion of the value of proposed actions and the desirability of the ends those actions may attain. Men persuade each other constantly that it is good to do x rather than y. But on the emotive account all we can do with others in such a dialogue is to incite them "to actions of one kind or another." And one wonders how people can have regular and predictable response to statements that have no meaning.

---

*Harcourt, Brace and Company, 3rd edition, 1930, p. 125.

There are two basic elements in statements of good and statements of right: the first is the knowledge of what is good and what is right; the second is the will to do them, which is a matter of socialization, emotion, and feelings of obligation. Neither is reducible to the other. We may know what is good or right and not want to do them, or we may want passionately to do what is good or right, but have no idea what to do, because we have no knowledge of good or right. We have a personal obligation to do whatever yields something we believe is good, and we have a social obligation to do what is right, or moral. The emotive theory is even more confused about the moral than about the good.

An emotive account of morals can explain felt obligation as a consequence of socialization, but it cannot thus explain obligation. An emotive doctrine may be a proper and informative adjunct to moral theory, but it is inadequate when it preempts the field: it locates obligation in the emotions of men instead of finding it, where it exists, in their society, with its institutions, associations, and other groups. It thus substitutes a frequent but not invariant concomitant of obligation for obligation itself, and it misstates a basic social process by confusing a way in which we are motivated with the reason why we are motivated in that way. It is essential to society that obligation be felt, but it must be genuine obligation which is felt, and that is discovered in observation and analysis.

When we do discover the conventional morals of groups we face other problems. The differing memberships (and statuses) of men, each with its own set of obligations, have different and even inconsistent ends. This inconsistency makes moral criticism imperative. Even a choice between contradictory obligations is tacit criticism, implying an order of rank among obligations. But we often do more than choose to fulfill one obligation rather than another: we try to change both so they become consistent. We may do this as members of the groups that have the obligations we find inconsistent, and we then appeal to the government of each group to make the change we propose. Or we may need the national government to make a decision that mediates among group claims and group obligations. That decision can be complicated by obligations derived from the nation itself, which may be inconsistent with those of groups within it. In such cases the national government must weigh its own claims and obligations against those of other groups. Such a procedure is not so arbitrary or so one-sided as it sounds, at least in democratic governments, because the judiciary bases its decisions on the arguments of lawyers, some of whom always represent individuals or groups, not the nation; and because the legislature is made up of representatives whose constituencies contain individuals and groups seeking and proposing changes.

Examples of obligation conflict between groups, including the nation-state, are everywhere. A family distinguishes its members from all others, creates love, and loyalty, and devotion, and excludes the rest of the world from its tight circle. Equally, members of a family share special obligations of care, nurture, and obedience. The nation, however, treats men as citizens or subjects, bound by the same laws and a common allegiance, subject to the same penalties, dedicated to national aims. Mothers do not send their sons to war happily, but the nation commands it; mothers have a basic obligation to provide for their children's welfare and the nation an obligation to its own safety. The conflict of obligations, even their disparity, has been noted through history, probed and dramatized in art, analyzed in philosophy. It is a conflict that requires moral criticism, and proposals for compromise, adjustment, and change. Curiously, the conflict of obligations within a society has not been a genuine subject for sociological study; should it become one, we could learn much.

And feelings of obligation when obligations conflict could be fertile ground for psychological study. As we internalize inconsistent obligations, we prepare the way for emotional disorder. We all live with intellectual inconsistencies readily enough, but when we feel the pull of opposed duties at a time when action must be of one kind or another there may be a crisis of conscience resulting in anguish, despair, or moral paralysis. Perhaps resolution of the difficulties of conscience best follows on intellectual solution of the conflict of obligation, and its practical resolution. But the problems themselves can be as bitter and painful as choice between obligation to a father and obligation to a mother.

Knowledge is of the greatest importance in solving the problems of conflicting obligation, and we would all benefit if the social sciences provided the kinds of knowledge we need. That knowledge would include such matters as a determination of the obligatory behavior expected of group members, the inconsistencies of obligation within a single group and among two or more groups, and the kinds of concrete situations in which behavior must be based on a choice between obligations or a compromise. Then, of course, there is the need to know how well each of the conflicting obligations is justified as a means for attaining its end, for if we must choose, we might well prefer a justified obligation to an unjustified one.

Informed choice in a situation of obligation conflict requires all this knowledge, and more. But we must not expect science or philosophy to provide a calculus of decision that can make a moral choice for us when the moment to choose comes. As in all other kinds of choice, the personality of the chooser, his experience, and the skill with which he handles practice are as basic to decision as knowledge of the consequences which follow from it. And no calculus can be responsible; some person always is. His skill is a moral art, which will always be required, even if we develop something like a moral science. That is not surprising, for analogies are commonplace: medical science, for instance, does not decide the treatment of a patient; the physician does.

Herbert W. Schneider has stated the case for a moral art extremely well.

Which of a number of alternative obligations is *the* duty to be performed in this situation is and should be determined on the spot (not in advance) in view of the particular importance of the competing obligations in this particular array of circumstances, not in view of a general, fixed list of priorities. Priorities vary with circumstances. The most rational decision is the most appropriate response to the situation, and this priority cannot be calculated either in advance or by fixed norms . . . . If, as in a game of chess, all the possible moves could be listed and all the rules were fixed and the number of possible situations were finite, it would be possible to refer 'the-right-move-in-this-situation' to a computer. But so long as life is not a closed game, so long must conscientious action involve a practical moral art: skill, experience, insight, imagination, cleverness, originality are all of them factors in right judgment. The best reason can do is to discipline each of these factors for what it is worth;

reason can never answer such problems independently of art,
nor conscience independently of experience. Responsibility is
achieved as it is in all the arts by learning the various skills
required. The road to acting responsibly is by learning the
hard way. Short cuts to moral knowledge are perilous.*

Society, as well as its members, suffers from its inconsistency and its conflicting pulls in obligation. Groups are chided and
weakened when their obligations are rejected in favor of obligations to other groups, for it is in the fulfillment of obligations by
their members that groups perform their functions (if the obligations are well calculated) and have their very being. Nothing else
can replace duty and the feeling of duty, the intellectual acceptance of obligation and the internalization of it in conscience.

Why implement decision through a feeling of obligation instead of simple command? There are several good reasons, one of
which, already stated, is that command without accepted and felt
obligation would probably involve an extensive use of force, and
even in despotisms force can be used effectively only in limited
ways and at great cost. A very simple example of the need for felt
obligation is that of an athletic group competing with another in a
tug-of-war. Especially if each of the groups is large, a member of
either of them may reason thus: Whether or not I pull on the rope
will probably make no difference to success or failure; why, then,
exert myself when I can pretend to pull without actually doing
so? Now it may actually be the case that whether or not this man
pulls will have no effect on the outcome. If his group wins he will
share in its glory although he did not contribute to its success.
And no great harm is done. But suppose several members of the
same group reasoned the same way? Success would, at least, be
jeopardized. And it is so easy to pretend to pull that the pre-
tenders might never be discovered. This risk of failure is minimized
when obligation to do what group decision demands is felt keenly.
In its simplest terms, obligation is fulfilled when one pulls one's
own weight. Thus, not only is the chance of success greater but
the rest of the membership does not incur a disproportionate
strain.

The process of what I have here called government is no

*Morals for Mankind, University of Missouri Press, 1960, pp. 19-20.

more immune from moral criticism than groups are, because part of the critical appraisal of obligations as means or functions is the way in which groups arrived at them. That is, we have not only the question whether given obligations do what they ought to do—and how well, and at what cost—but the question of legitimacy. A good decision made illegitimately may reasonably be rejected at times, and a poor decision made legitimately accepted, because the process of decision-making or the setting of precedent may be more important than a particular decision. In a common instance, a higher court may overrule a lower because of the way it made its decision, even if the decision seems correct.

There are many reasons to be more concerned with legitimacy and procedure than with particular results. One is obvious. When we think that the process we approve for decision-making works better than others, we are likely to guard the process jealously, and to reject decisions we would otherwise accept, because of the way they were made. Discussion of such matters is, I know, a staple of political, rather than moral, theory but what is emerging from this argument, I hope, is that political theory is a part of moral philosophy or, since pride of place is of little intellectual significance, that each is always properly involved with the other.

The transformation of existing morality into reflective morality by an unremitting process of criticism is even more basic than I have yet suggested, since it includes the task of dealing rationally with the functional prerequisites of society. There are perhaps no structures necessary to society but there are necessary social functions, those without which there can be no society. People living together must, first of all, live. They must have ways of acquiring and distributing necessities of life, like food and shelter. And since people live together, there must be organized ways of acquiring and distributing commodities, and of allocating and using resources, in short, an economy. Merely to continue to live may also require protection, not just from animals and weather, but from other men. Internal and external security may or may not be important under the circumstances of the moment, but when they are important they lead to official force, judgment or mediation of disputes, and rule.

For a society to remain identifiably the same society, even

with some change from one generation to the next, there must be a transmission of the culture of the older generation to the younger. This is the root function of education. To give a sense of community, to weld society into some unity, there must be common norms and beliefs, which in the past have been provided or supported by religion. In order that men cooperate for shared ends, including protection of life and property, morality must permeate the society. A slightly different case can be made for the necessity of art, and I shall not attempt it here. Government and law, though, are needed to ensure that men do what it is thought they should, and not do what it is thought they should not, to coordinate different human activities, and to make decisions for society.

Functional theory in social science includes, I think rightly, the belief that social prerequisites of a functional sort are fixed, but the structures which perform those functions are variable. Monogamy, polygamy, and polyandry are all forms of the family, and perform its functions. The forms of institutional and group structure found in any society are not themselves necessary—there are exceptions to this—to its mere survival as a society, although their functions are. But the different structural forms are basic to the culture and ethos of each society, and though a society still exists when other structural forms are substituted for them, it may not be the same society. Much of that culture and ethos (the social quality or spirit) is changed when, for example, polygamy is replaced by monogamy.

All these structural forms are organized groups which develop codes of obligation specifying the conduct expected of members so that functional prerequisites can be served. It is organized human conduct, not reified social entities, that does this job, which is indispensable to social life. And that conduct is required by duty. Thus morals are born from the womb of necessity.

Yet the obligations demanded may be ill calculated; they may not in fact serve functional needs, or may not serve them well. Here, clearly, is a fundamental source of moral criticism. To go even further: there is also the question whether other social structures (monogamy rather than polygamy, democracy rather than monarchy) are needed to alter existent obligation so it does serve functional needs. Structures and obligations are so closely woven that a significant change in obligation might entail a change in structure, as changes in structure entail changes in obligation. When men are no longer obligated only to obey the law, for example, but also to participate in deciding it, the political machinery must change to accommodate the new obligation, becoming republican, perhaps, instead of despotic.

On another level, there is the question of maintaining the culture and its ethos, not just society. One of the obligations we bear to each group is the general one of ensuring its continuance. And loyalty, social inertia, and particular beliefs tend to make us preservers not just of the group, but of its cultural detail. Here moral criticism is necessary to appraise that cultural detail, find its bearings on obligation and shared ends, and deal with the complex problems of loyalty and inertia. The furniture of a culture becomes a way of life; some prefer it to all other furniture, seen and unseen, tried and untried. Yet it creates an unwitting ethos, a spirit and quality that is admirable or ignoble, in the end affecting our obligations and our will to fulfill them.

As examples: a well-to-do class, with few admitted burdens, in a pleasant climate where innocent and not-so-innocent pleasures abound, may be willing to fight to maintain its privileges but unwilling to bother with real social needs, and still more unwilling to make sacrifices to meet them. An aristocracy of labor leaders, well-paid and well-treated, looking for all the world like the business magnates with whom they negotiate, may lose a sense of obligation to the workers they are supposed to represent. Those workers, in turn, with good jobs, relative security, and considerable leisure may regard the world as turned upside down if they are asked to include in their midst a different ethnic group, trying to escape from poverty. The labor union loses its purpose and becomes a club of the labor elite; the business community forgets its obligations to those it employs and those it should employ, and seals itself off from them. This is fertile soil for the moralist, and even more for the social critic with an eye for the psychic and moral consequences of the ordinary ways of life. Such critics are rare and should be cherished; they deal in matters most people do not even notice and seek connections only proven in later times.

When criticism moves on from cultural ethos to personal life

it has a more definite subject, though still a difficult one. Part of
the difficulty is the pursuit of happiness, ever involved in our
concern for personal values. We are not asked, except in heroic
moments, for utter self-sacrifice, and we should not be, for life is
not entirely obligation and men need opportunity to pursue advantage and value. Recurrently, duty and advantage clash, but for the
moral philosopher that clash is less interesting than the way in
which social obligation, derived from status, impinges on the person. Although obligation holds because of status, it is felt by
persons. Also, as I have argued, there is an axiological obligation
for the person to do the things that yield his values, and to carry
out voluntary personal commitments. Between felt social obligation and axiological obligation there can be conflict that rends the
psyche. There is no obligation, however, to seek our own advantage, although most of us demand a sphere in which we can do so.
Usually that sphere is thought of as private, disconnected from the
public sphere of duty. But for all one's desire for a completely
private sphere which could offer genuine moral holidays, we find
the private realm invaded at almost every point by social obligation.

There is no reason, it might seem, that a man should not
regularly get drunk in the privacy of his own home, if that is what
he likes to do, but what is the effect of such conduct on his
family, his friends, and his job? A man is entitled, one wants to
say, to amuse himself in any way that does not hurt others. But
what kind of person does he make himself by those amusements?
Is it a person capable of fulfilling his obligations? The key to the
question is the effect personal and private behavior has on moral
conduct. What we do is an expression of what we are, but it also
makes us what we will be. And the person one becomes acts in his
statuses as a moral agent beset by problems of obligation. So there
is an ancillary obligation that falls on each person: to make himself capable of fulfilling obligation. Indeed, what he does in the
personal sphere often bears directly on his obligation. If he trifles
with his health, for instance, even for the sake of something valuable, he may hurt his wife, his children, and the causes in which
he is enlisted. His values, then, must be shaped by knowledge of
his actual and potential obligations, as his obligations must be
accepted or rejected in accordance with his values and, if accepted,

criticized in their terms. Value and morality are distinguishable, and much that can be said of one cannot be said of the other, but in the end they interact.

Knowledge of the relations between the personal and the public spheres is relevant to still another area of critical morality, appraisal of shared ends and purposes, and of the groups that presumably yield them. We need not criticize obligatory means only; we may also judge ends, for they should be derived from shared and consistent values. Values are more general than ends, and are realized in their more particular embodiments. Such values as health and pleasure may be served by joining an athletic club whose ends are playing certain games. But if the games are over-strenuous, and lead to large numbers of physical injuries, and if they are played with a strenuous, even grim, desire to win, neither of the values is realized. Too commonly, the shared ends that justify membership in a group do not in fact serve the values that in turn justify the ends. I have not argued that shared values justify membership (only that shared ends, plus other conditions, do), because people with different values may choose the same ends, each sure that his own values are thus served. If A values health, and B pleasure, and C social contacts, all three may join a country club whose end is playing golf. And each may thus serve a different value by an identical end. Yet there are circumstances in which the end serves some values and not others, circumstances in which it serves none of the values for which it was selected, and circumstances in which it serves values not originally intended.

That groups continue to exist even when the ends they attain have little connection with their members' values is not surprising; thoughtlessness and social inertia account for a good deal, and genuine moral criticism is rare. But one interesting situation is occasionally noted, though seldom analyzed: organizations, sometimes continuing the same functions, cease to serve the values they once did, and begin to serve other values. An important instance is, I think, the United Nations, whose activities have little of their original, or intended value, and almost no practical effect, but become symbolic of world interest and national concern. The United Nations Assembly has less and less chance of keeping peace or repressing aggression, but increasingly provides a forum where national policies find a world audience. Perhaps the United Nations would never have been created for these purposes, but it already exists and its machinery can be put to the service of values not originally connected to its ends. Thoroughgoing moral criticism of it might again justify its existence, although for new reasons, or conclude that it is unjustifiable, or suggest alternatives, but most criticism has been self-serving.

Knowledge of the personal sphere bears on the public sphere in more than the relation of values to obligations. There are always questions about the wisdom of having Mr. A in a given status, because of his ability or inability to fulfill the obligations that devolve upon that status. Such questions are particular and have few implications for social structure or moral obligation unless they are broadened to ask also about the procedures by which Mr. A acquired his status. Procedures of appointment and promotion, for example, have a moral dimension because they are relevant to the fulfillment of obligation, and so to the attainment of group ends. Inefficient or venal methods of filling posts may lead an entire organization to moral disorder. Efficient and honest methods require knowledge of the abilities of all the Mr. A's who might fill the posts.

Of course, we are also concerned with Mr. A, not just the post he serves. We want him treated justly and well, at least some of us do, and we have organized our procedures so he should be treated that way. Perhaps our most important values are involved, they lead to ends we share, and they in turn to procedures which are means to those ends. Not every group is made up of members with such values prominent in their minds and hearts, and in consequence some groups favor the strong and ruthless and protect others little if at all. One important reason for getting group acceptance of fair and honorable treatment of all members is that, even though we want everyone treated justly and well, we ordinarily bother ourselves for people we like and overlook unjust treatment of people we don't like. Sometimes we positively enjoy injustice done our enemies. It is group function, when it works well, that brings equality of treatment to its members.

From Mr. A's point of view, there is need for him to know personal things that can help decide whether to seek or accept a particular status. He may be psychically unsuited to it, or may court corruption because of the status's nature and his own. Also, some of us never learn that if we take on too many obligations (those that are not inescapable), we cannot do justice to any of them. We should accept them only if they lead to ends we strongly approve, and if we are capable of fulfilling the obligations themselves. Our capability can be determined by examining ourselves; many people cannot meet even the minimal obligations of marriage. But there is also the larger study—one that could be made by the social sciences—which would match the norms and values of the members of a group or society (measuring them apart from group membership and statuses) with what are thought to be the purposes of the groups they belong to, and their consequent obligations as members and occupiers of particular statuses. Such studies could yield some idea of the level of integration in any society and help pinpoint areas of disintegration.

Our search for critical morality will never be ended. We cannot arrive at a fixed morality in which we can finally rest because changing circumstances alter the relations of means and ends, and circumstances continue to change. In the ideal case, the ends of a group are shared by all its members and accord with their values, the best means to those ends are the obligations of the members, and they are coordinated efficiently. But were an ideal case to exist it, too, would suffer the effects of change. For new circumstances can make it impossible for the means of the group, however splendidly they once worked, now to yield their ends. Just as a college class in contemporary history must weigh every new occurrence to see whether its effects are great enough to warrant its inclusion in their study so, ideally, new circumstances should be judged for their relevance to group obligation and purpose. In fact, we are often so far behind the circumstances of our own time that our conventional obligations defeat the purposes they are intended to serve. This is an area of moral criticism of such importance that I shall consider it separately in the next chapter.

I assume I have neglected many ways in which conventional morals can be criticized, but I do not want to overlook what strikes some as the chief way: the criticism based on what we owe the largest group, mankind. This is not identical with the absolute morality or the natural law discussed earlier, for it need not be absolute; it may even have the same form as the social obligation I have discussed, but its obligations are regarded as the fundamental obligations.

What may be most plausible about this is a hidden analogy to groups within a society. Smaller groups may be members of larger groups, and they members of still larger, until all are contained within the nation-state, which makes decisions for the entire society, and mediates among all groups. When two groups are members of, or contained within, a larger group, they share obligations within it which have some priority. If A and B are political parties with members in a parliament, then the parliamentary members of both parties have obligations to the parliament which take precedence over the obligations owed to the parties. If they regard obligations to A and B as prior, they may destroy parliament and with it, perhaps, A and B, for those will lose their basic purpose, to elect members to parliament.

So with all groups which join in larger groupings: the new association creates new obligations which are basic, first, to its own continuance and, second, to the continuance or welfare of the smaller groups within it. Why not, then, continue the inclusion of the smaller within the larger until all are contained within mankind? Or perhaps (we may argue, in a way both simpler and more appealing), in whatever other groups men are associated, they are all members of mankind and should take that natural necessity as basic to morality.

But there is no mankind. "Man" is a word for a logical class or a biological species, like "horse," not for an association. Human sympathy with other humans is an endearing trait, but it does not convert the class, man—all men, past, present, and future—into an association. Mankind, in that sense, does not exist, although one of our most important tasks is to create it, for we are not, and cannot be, safe in our other associations until we create mankind. We have taken many small steps in the right direction. They include international courts, Grotius's laws of war, the League of Nations, the United Nations, treaties, and trade. Some of those steps needed greater preliminaries, and some have little more than propaganda value, but they were steps. Still, almost all of us have obligations to all other men anyway, even in the absence of mankind. It does not take a universal morality based on the family, or association, of man for those all-important obligations to exist.

We owe our obligations to behave in certain ways to all men by virtue of membership in less universal groups that create those obligations. Of these, the most important are religions. If a religion holds to the ideal of the brotherhood of man, its purpose is promoted by creating obligations toward all men. Many who cannot fully accept existing churches do accept some of their moral doctrine. It is as if they felt themselves members of an ideal religion, existing only in a Platonic heaven, whose laws they must obey. Judeo-Christian and other religions have persuaded multitudes of the charity with which they should behave to all. So with believers in absolute secular moralities, with bases like Nature, Human Nature, and the Structure of Reason. I may not believe these yield genuine obligations, but much of the world does.

As for mankind, regarded as an association of all men, it does not yet exist but it can indeed be created. Although men do not start with a universal morality, they can come to it. The obvious way, through world government, has many dangers, and should probably be built as the culmination of a long process of making ties and bonds throughout the world. Necessity, though, may dictate world government first, or nothing. If we do come to it, our universal obligations will be primary but few, in comparison to the multiplicity of obligations to smaller groups. And we need not regret that those universal obligations were not there from the beginning. Critical morality is man's achievement, not his master.

CHAPTER SIX

The Limits of Consensus

When men change the ends they share as members of a group, reason requires that they change the obligations that yield those ends. When the ends are retained, but new conditions make existent obligations poor, useless, or wrong as means, men should criticize, and again change them. It is hard for people to alter their obligations rationally, even under the best conditions, but as the rate of change increases dizzily in our day, the problems become more confusing and the need more urgent. I want, therefore, to consider how we can change obligations deliberately.

For the moment, but for the moment only, let us put aside the question of motivating people to fulfill their obligations. Not everyone who accepts an obligation intellectually feels it keenly enough to act on it, and moral exhortation is an appeal to the emotions to elicit action. The world is full of moral exhortation because it is full of people who don't do what some others expect of them. But the world is also full of people—even the same people—who do much that is expected of them. And the problem that concerns me here is based on the latter case: what is the result of people's continuing to do what they feel as obligatory even when that ought to be changed? Moralists worry that people do not feel the obligations they accept, and so are not motivated to act on them. And that is often the case. But it is also the case that many are over-motivated, over-socialized with respect to morality, and so are incapable of change when the time for change comes. This is the problem of the twelfth criterion of critical morality, stated in the fifth chapter.

There is normally some chance, however slight, of altering

obligation deliberately, even in societies without despotic power structures; people are seldom so rigid as to be entirely immovable about what they believe and feel to be right. But moral beliefs and norms are usually firm enough that they can be changed only within severe limits. Some consensus is required for change to be accepted, and at any time there are extremes beyond which consensus cannot be moved. I shall call those extremes the limits of consensus.

When one proposes a change in conduct, to meet a new situation perhaps, he is normally bound within the limits of consensus and finds himself with no one to listen or care, if he has exceeded the limits substantially. The only chance for his proposal comes when something alters the limits. Tentatively, a generalization can be made that when a social situation is stable, the limits of consensus change only in the slow round of time, but in crisis the limits may contract or expand greatly, and sometimes swiftly. The extremes of expansion and contraction are found in revolution and reaction.

The more deeply we feel obligations the less likely we are to tamper with the limits of consensus even in crisis, although much is at stake. We cry *Fiat iustitia, pereat mundus,* and watch the world burn. The graver the crisis, though, the greater our fears and anxieties and the more the chance that we stretch our limits wide or shrink them narrow. The tension between deeply felt obligation and the terrors of crisis is great, and proposals for change must be marvelously apt if they can resolve the crisis and yet gain acceptance. Sometimes no proposal can do both.

In a nation that ends a war with its young men slaughtered but its young women for the most part unhurt, there is the serious problem of replenishing the stock. It has been suggested that the dreadful losses among the best young men in World War I destroyed the possibility of successful leadership in France and Germany for more than a generation after the peace, and resulted in the instability of the French Republic and the horrors of the Third Reich. Suppose that, foreseeing such possibilities, a law had been introduced in the Chamber of Deputies or the Reichstag to make polygamy legal. Its advocates might point out that the law would encourage the finest and most vigorous of the young men who survived to marry plurally and infuse the nation with their genes. To that end a subsidy might be proposed only for the best young veterans. What would the response have been? Probably derision. Could a matter like the future of the nation weigh heavily enough to end monogamy, which is the form of marriage God desires for his children? Most unlikely.

Yet in World War II, when France's defenses were overrun and the country could no longer be held against the Germans, Winston Churchill asked the French to fight on from North Africa, and offered Frenchmen British citizenship, while retaining their own. The limits of consensus in Britain were thus assumed to have expanded radically under the threat of destruction, although we cannot be sure they had. In France it was too late for the offer to mean much although, had it been accepted, Europe might be entirely different today. Think of the years in which France excluded Britain from the Common Market. In crisis, one must act at the right time; second chances are not guaranteed.

These two examples make it seem that the obligations most difficult to change are those of the smaller, functionally prerequisite groups invested with the deepest emotions; and that might very well be so. But the emotions attending nationalism are nonetheless powerful, as international relations attest. The question I want to ask is what, apart from habituation, creates the inertia that keeps inadequate obligation alive and resists change, however useful?

The answer, I think, has to do with the initial problem of motivating people to perform obligatory acts. Basic to that are the expectations and responses of others, internalization of those expectations in conscience, the promise of reward for fulfillment, and the threat of punishment for nonfulfillment. We are habituated so that accepted obligation becomes, to some extent, felt obligation, because we are raised to believe that we ought to do what we accept as right. But I am suggesting that all this is often not enough, especially for some people. Those who need additional reinforcement include two important types: what we may call the Machiavellians, those who do not want to pull on the rope, or fulfill their obligations, because the ends they share will probably be attained for them by others who do fulfill their obligations; and what we may call the skeptics, those who do not fully accept their obligations because they are not persuaded that they really are obligations.

There is some difference in the ways of getting both Machiavellians and skeptics to feel their obligations, and so be motivated to fulfill them; and coercion may be more necessary in dealing with Machiavellians than with skeptics. One difference between them, after all, is that the Machiavellian may know what his obligations are, but not feel them, while the skeptic does not accept his obligations at all, or at least has doubts about them. The skeptic may still fulfill his obligations out of custom; the Machiavellian is of course a man who tries to escape the thorns of obligation while enjoying its fruits. Machiavellians may have to be treated individually, except for the general threat of reprisal when caught. Skeptics, though, make their problem one of belief, and may be able to feel obligations when they have accepted them.

Historically, custom, religion, and reverence for the ancient ways are sufficient for a time to get obligation fulfilled. When the breakdown of tradition occurs, as it did so dramatically in ancient Greece in the generation of Socrates and Euripides, reason and argument are needed, or a new faith. Unwilling to do things simply because they are customary, men then need intellectual persuasion or religious conversion before they accept obligation, old or new. Even devoutly religious men at certain times question obligations demanded by their religions, as they doubt some of its tenets. That is the situation of many devout Roman Catholics today who question their church's stand on birth control. Intellectual religious doubt requires theology, as do questions about religious obligation. Secular doubt, too, may be satisified by theology, if theology's mantle casts a long enough shadow, and if the community as a whole is religious.

Skepticism, as I am using the word, does not mean a denial of the possibility of truth; it means unwillingness to accept what is ordinarily called true or right, and a search for evidence or justification. In this sense, skepticism is dissipated when acceptable answers are found. The usual answers to "Why ought we to do x?" have not been of the kind I have offered, perhaps because that kind of answer has not been understood, although it seems to underlie the facts of morality. But were it offered, it still might not do the job of getting men to feel their obligations, because it is straightforward and rational, and that rarely arouses strong emotion. Especially in the case of the Machiavellian, my kind of answer might only support his tendency to reap the rewards of others' labors. But the skeptic, too, would be challenged to behave reasonably, in cooperation with others, for the attainment of shared ends. And his skepticism might not be fully eradicated, for he would still have the arduous task of moving to a critical morality. Indeed, since a critical morality, as I conceive it, is never finished, the certainty and finality in which most skeptics would like to rest are removed as possibilities.

The answers to "Why ought we to do x," if they are to persuade skeptics, should offer absolutes, certainties, and finalities; and they should also arouse reverence, awe, and dedication if they are to reinforce the feeling of obligation. In a religious community, it may take no more to create accepted obligation than persuasive theological argument, and no more than that for felt obligation, too, because theology is invested with religious commitment. But increasing secularization weakens the persuasiveness of theology, while at the same time growing education increases the persuasiveness of philosophy.

Highly educated men, like the *philosophes* of the Enlightenment, are—or were—persuaded by philosophical argument, and are very likely to internalize the morality they accept. It is a trait of most educated men that they believe, defend, and act out what they accept as true; their characters have been so formed by their education. But in matters of morals—and political philosophy—commitment must run deep, and it is bolstered by powerful appeals, no longer to the will of God, perhaps, but to things like nature and nature's laws, the constitution of human nature, or the structure of reason. The social contract was, to some of its adherents, just rational agreement among men, on a commercial analogue, about what would benefit all. (Here, I think, there is almost a model of agreeing on shared ends, erecting a social structure to attain them, and accepting as obligation or law that structure's decisions on conduct that will attain those ends.) But to other adherents the contract took the form of the ancient covenant of Adam and Abraham with God, and had overtones of religion, not commerce.

The social contract, like God's will, nature, and the other traditional appeals of morals and politics, has been a base for particular judgments and an antecedent of correct decision, an antecedent immemorial and revered. And for some it was not a contract of the moment among the living only, to be altered whenever the parties to it claimed it no longer provided the benefits it should, and perhaps once did. It was, in Burke's rhetoric, ". . . . a partnership not only between those who are living, but between those who are living, those who are dead, and those who are to be born." So the contract was part rational, part traditional, part commercial, and part religious. It served its purposes, as the other bases did and, like them, revealed somewhat the social functions of philosophy.

In secular societies, philosophy has functioned as a surrogate for theology and religion in justifying the norms and obligations of the day. If we won't do A because we are told it is the will of God and we don't believe in God or don't believe God's will is known, we may still do the identical A if a philosophical base justifies it. We may not grant that the world is a perfect whole because God created it as such, but we may accept the same thesis because it is justified by Absolute Idealism.

One of the social functions of philosophy, as of ideology and religion, has been to foster stability, and so to hinder change. Yet we need far more historical and social study of the function of ideas under different conditions than we have, for it is quite evident that, again like religion and ideology, there are times when philosophy promotes change and even revolution. To be sure, the philosophers themselves make a difference, and there may have been times with little stability and yet no revolution, because there was not a philosopher of great enough powers to increase the one or stimulate the other.

As instances of religion and philosophy in the service of revolution: Cromwell's armies made puritan theology a weapon of revolt and church practice a basis for new political forms. Lord Lindsay maintained for years that democracy was born of puritanism and lost its *raison d'être* if it forgot puritan ideas. And of more secular thought, Otto Gierke said: "The Law of Nature issued in a natural-law theory of the State; and it was by developing such a theory that it affected the movement of history most powerfully . . . . In opposition to positive jurisprudence, which still continued to show a Conservative trend, the natural-law theory of the State was Radical to the very core of its being."*

Yet after revolution the old problems of stability return. The new social structure, or the one men hope for, has its morality as much as the old, and new obligation, to be deeply felt, needs a justification that is stirring, because custom and tradition are missing. But ancient warrants are often introduced in support of the new dispensation, as in. the case of Cromwell. And others are common enough: we have watered the pure milk of the original doctrine, we are told, we have strayed from the path of the Founding Fathers, or we must return to the old religion—usually in a new guise.

Whether reactionary or revolutionary, whether in de Maistre or Rousseau, another function of religion, ideology, and philosophy has been to make us feel at home in the universe by making nature and history intelligible, and then to articulate or create obligations, and to get them accepted and felt. When all the other factors are added to the internalization of obligation—custom, tradition, coercion, socialization—there is a kind of moral overkill: some people feel their obligations so keenly and regard their moral base as so evident and certain, that they are not able to act rationally in moral matters to change what needs to be changed. Equally, when new and revolutionary obligations are philosophically based and formulated, and are then reinforced by the sentiments and ideals of the day, it is difficult to the point of impossibility to persuade people that some things should not be changed or changed much.

The limits of consensus, based on felt obligation, thus become a part of the problem of stability versus flexibility in social groups and in society itself: depending on whether the limits remain or alter, they hinder or foster change, including moral change. Moral change occurs with all other social change and interacts with it: e.g., important changes in obligation usually require changes in social structure, and structural changes require moral changes. But consensual limits may be different for conduct and for avowal of that conduct, making flexibility greater in action than in speech, or vice versa. Society often copes with the need

*Natural Law and the Theory of Society, tr. by Ernest Barker, Beacon Press, 1957, p. 35

for new morality by a standard hypocrisy that permits new types of conduct while verbally upholding antithetical obligations. Sexual relations are an obvious instance. Sometimes the limits are wider for speech than for action. Revolutionary utterances may be permitted but revolutionary action suppressed.

Stability may be thought of as the continuance of the group in all its basic forms, with its detail largely unaltered. Flexibility is the ability of the group to change its detail and its obligations, when change is needed, in order to maintain the group's essential nature, its values, its ends, its functions, and the ability to change ends if they no longer accord with values. Crisis may alter the group's very nature when, for example, the lives of the members are threatened, or the national entity would otherwise disappear. In our day, the satellites of the Soviet Union have undergone such alteration. The French and Russian revolutions changed the nature of each nation, as the Turkish elimination of polygamy changed its institution of marriage fundamentally. There is still, in such changes, some continuity—of language, custom, and function, for example—and so the same group in some ways, but greatly altered. When there is a change in values, implemented by changes in structure and ends, revolution has taken place. And, of course, when all continuity has ended, the group has been destroyed, probably to be replaced by a new group. Let us deal with stability and flexibility first.

A group with great stability and little flexibility may function splendidly in the absence of crisis, but be altered in essentials by great pressures when crisis comes. A group with great flexibility and little stability may be mobile and changeable without crisis, sometimes to the point of dysfunction, but capable of maintaining its essential nature by imagination and controlled change when crisis occurs. Monogamous marriage in the west, for example, unstable in its divorce rate and the fidelity of its partners, has been maintained in its essentials, although with many changes in the detail of family life, under the pressure of poverty and wealth, industrialization, the move of populations from rural to urban and then to suburban areas, and economies which brought sometimes earlier and sometimes later marriages.

Every group is stable in some ways and flexible in others, but as a whole, in respect to group continuance, some groups have an advantage in stability, and some in flexibility. What usually brings these advantages, sometimes with compensating disadvantages, is the structure of group decision and enforcement. Decisions made by one man can be quicker, for example, than decisions made by parliamentary bodies representing varied and opposing interests. Group decisions backed by force can be more surely enacted than those carried out by conscience. The factors involved in decision and execution include government, group integration, and consent. All governments, of course, rest on some consent, or at least acquiescence, but governments, or perhaps groups themselves, with their ends and means, can be classified in their actions as resting more on force or more on commitment. And group decision can be classified as based more on custom or more on reason.

To apply these two distinctions to stability and flexibility: groups dependent on force tend to make decisions based on reason rather than custom. Reason is probably not the right word here, for reason embraces thought about ends and values, as well as thought about means; rational manipulation of means is closer to what I mean. Force, or the threat of force, can overcome the inertia of custom, and permit manipulation outside the consensual limits custom provides, thus yielding flexibility. Dictatorships make sudden shifts in policy when that seems useful. Groups dependent on commitment are most likely, when they escape custom, to base their decisions on reason in a fuller sense than that of manipulation, because their government is more responsible to the members of its group and must justify its decisions to them. On the other hand, such groups are usually more bound by custom and can move less readily outside the limits of consensus, thus yielding a greater stability.

Both types of group, those dependent on force and those dependent on commitment, can be classified on a custom-reason scale, with the qualifications that have been made about the meaning of "reason." An authoritarian group in a religious age may depend heavily on custom, and rarely move outside the usual limits of consensus; but an authoritarian group not held by such ties has a leadership freer to decide and act than the leadership of groups based on commitment.

When a group is authoritarian, and depends on force, its

leaders may move with a speed that is rare in a group whose action in crisis requires a new consensus on the part of committed members. The Soviet-Nazi Pact, for instance, was announced so suddenly as to astonish the world; the residents of Moscow, who had gone to bed the night before with phrases about Fascist beasts in their ears, were told one morning to cheer as Ribbentrop was driven through their streets with swastikas flying from his car. It is almost inconceivable that the same thing could have happened in England or America at that time.

A group based greatly on force has the same advantage in flexibility that law has as compared with morals, or articulated morals as compared with unformulated or implicit morals. One may add that it is like the advantage in flexibility that politics has in contrast with the greater stability of society. The contrast in each case is partly the difference between what has been formulated, brought to consciousness, and so is corrigible, and the unarticulated but latent. Thus it is a contrast between what is deliberately, or rationally, brought about, and what is not. In nondeliberate change, like social change that occurs without being instigated or controlled, the tempo is more continuous, the change is usually unnoticed until it is fairly great, and its probable consequences are not immediately clear. In deliberate change, the tempo is, in comparison, abrupt and fitful, the change is readily noticed, and the intended consequences may be fairly obvious. As an example of articulated and deliberate change, the Nineteenth Amendment to the United States Constitution, granting women the vote, although discussed and debated for years, abruptly changed the nature of citizenship for women and doubled the size of the vote. The growth in crime, however, much as the news media make of it today, went unnoticed for years. Changes due to increased crime are great, especially in large cities, and apart from making parks and night streets unsafe, crime once noticed has become a political issue strong enough to seat or unseat public officials. Uninstigated as deliberate policy, unguided by any agency, increased crime when noticed and studied brings deliberate change in law, law enforcement, and municipal regulations. And the intentional change brought about by the Nineteenth Amendment had, as a movement in the other direction, unintended consequences in liberating women from the home and sending them to schools and jobs. I will treat this movement from the intended to the unintended, and back again, in a different context in Chapter Nine.

Consensual limits may vary greatly from one to another region of the same society, so that a national consensus on deliberate change may not be enough to ensure effective administration of the change through the entire nation. In addition, unintended and unforeseen consequences of deliberate change may arouse resistance even in those who supported the change. Instances are everywhere.

In one example of social versus political change: educational desegregation in the United States moved like a snail until a Supreme Court decision altered the situation abruptly, and brought it to the attention of the nation. Immediately there were changes, some frantic, which were given wide publicity. But the limits of consensus had not been considered, especially in the South, and great expectations were dashed as segregation was, although greatly lessened, not eliminated with the speed so many had expected. In addition there were unintended consequences, like the need to send children by bus to schools not in their own neighborhood, and unforeseen consequences like a demand for segregation by some militant blacks. A result was anger and bloodshed. As for the Soviet-Nazi Pact, that was international and depended for its success on the response of other nations; it ended in war between the two parties, and a sudden shift in alliances. This is not to deprecate planned change, but to show its difficulties when consensus does not exist.

An authoritarian group has even more flexibility than the analogues cited in the discussion of groups based on force: law, articulated morals, politics (in a democratic society). Those are flexible in comparison with morals, unformulated morals, and society, but still require more discussion and time before changes are made than is the case in an authoritarian group. The problem of acting speedily in crisis thus plagues and weakens democratic nations when they are in a power-struggle with authoritarian nations. They may have an advantage of their own in the matter of flexibility, however, when the dependence of group decision on custom or reason is considered, but I will leave that for the next chapter. It is the relation of flexibility to force and commitment that I want to treat now.

The government of any group can act outside the limits of consensus on occasion. Just as, in a previous instance, consensus can be one thing for speech and another for action, so it can be one thing for acceptance and another for acquiescence, however grudging. We may not accept, or consent to, behavior or legislation to which we may still acquiesce, because the consequences of opposition may seem worse than the consequences of acquiescence. Franco's choice of a successor did not seem to have the consent of the Spanish people, but the consequence of opposition was probably civil war. The significance of the limits of consensus for action is relative to the political structure of the group: the more authoritarian the group the less limited it is by consensus, because acceptance is less necessary to action; the more participatory—democratic?—the group, the more limited it is by consensus, although by no means totally limited. The tyrannical father, in a culture that supports his tyranny, can make capricious decisions affecting his children's futures, without consulting them or his wife; and the family will usually obey. Acceptance is a somewhat different matter than obedience, which results from acquiescence. Some of the children may accept the decision in time, but not with the alacrity with which they obey it. Some may never accept, and yet still obey. So with the wife. And so with Soviet citizens at the time of the Soviet-Nazi Pact.

That democratic national governments, too, act outside the limits of consensus may be seen by examination of public opinion polls. Many criticisms can be made of the polls as they are used now, but they do reflect a constantly shifting consensus, within its ordinary limits, when there is no crisis. When the polls show responses to the decisions of government, it becomes apparent how and when the government acts outside the limits of consensus, how far outside it gets—not nearly so far, nor so fast, as authoritarian government can—and to what extent governmental action changes consensual limits by bringing acceptance that did not exist initially. Parliamentary government, based on a system of political parties, has an unusual opportunity to alter the limits of consensus somewhat, even in the absence of great crisis. Its parties, seeking election, have a public forum, their ideas are presented in almost every home on almost every day, and the prestige of a few leaders weighs heavily in public consideration of issues. Immensely popular leaders can sometimes alter widespread attitudes, but the history of democratic politics illustrates what usually happens to even the most popular leaders who stray too far or too often outside the momentary limits of consensus.

In a republican government, the "rulers" are in a complex relation to the "ruled." Responsibility to the electorate is enforced by the decisions of the voting booth. But currying favor with the people, although indispensable to success in a free election, is not the fundamental task of those who are elected, or at least, however they behave, not the proper task. They must make decisions for the electorate that they, who have power, think are best for it. The question is whether the "ruler" is a delegate, doing what his constituents decide, or a representative, guarding the interests of the constituency according to his own judgment, while remembering, and placing first, the welfare of the whole.

Edmund Burke, in his election speech of November 3, 1774, told the voters of Bristol:

> Certainly, Gentlemen, it ought to be the happiness and glory of a representative to live in the strictest union, the closest correspondence, and the most unreserved communication with its constituents. Their wishes ought to have great weight with him; their opinions high respect; their business unremitted attention. It is his duty to sacrifice his repose, his pleasure, his satisfaction to theirs—and above all, ever, to prefer their interest to his own.
>
> But his unbiased opinion, his mature judgment, his enlightened conscience, he ought not to sacrifice to you, to any man, or to any set of men living. These he does not derive from your pleasure—no, nor from the law and constitution . . . . Your representative owes you, not his industry only, but his judgment; and he betrays, instead of serving you, if he sacrifices it to your opinion.
>
> . . . government and legislation are matters of reason and judgment, and not inclination; and what sort of reason is that in which the determination precedes the discussion, in which one set of men deliberate and another decide, and where those who form the conclusion are perhaps three hundred miles distant from those who hear the arguments.

For all his veneration of tradition and custom, Burke moved deliberately outside the limits of consensus among his constituents. The limits to legislation, in his own mind, were those of reform, as distinct from innovation, because innovation on a national scale seemed to him possible only by first destroying the old, and so became revolution. But reform, when needed, was the legislator's task; the constituent's task was to understand the reasons for the reform, judge its effectiveness, and widen the limits of consensus to accommodate it. If he could not or would not do those things, or if the reform remained unacceptable to him, he could refuse to return the legislator to office.

Burke spoke for a parliamentary government, with guarantees of liberty for its citizens. Entirely different principles animate despotic government, and it faces different problems with its subjects than Burke did with his constituents. There is a direct proportion between force and flexibility, and an inverse proportion between commitment or persuasion and flexibility. Despotism can move outside consensual limits much more readily than democracy, and can move farther. In our day democratic governments that act with restraint toward violent dissenters, who are among those to whom government is responsible, can have great trouble repressing riots and even preventing assassination. Despotisms are unlikely to act with restraint and can more easily preserve civil peace, even if it is the peace of the dead. Insurrection is almost impossible today so long as government controls the battalions and will act ruthlessly, massively, and quickly. Barricades can fend off only cavalry, not tanks; houses can hold back infantry, not artillery and planes. When the major weapons of a time are easily procurable or cheaply made without great technical skill, civilians can get them and insurrection is possible; when major weapons are not procurable by civilians and are very costly and technically difficult to make, insurrection against a ruthless modern nation is almost without chance.

Insurrection is an extreme response to a situation in which many people no longer share the ends of important institutions backed by national force, or in which the obligatory means to those ends seem hopelessly wrong to people who may not even dare to say so, let alone try to change them peacefully. Personal values then take precedence over social obligations; or else the new

institutions planned by revolutionaries for the future, with new
and different obligations, then become the objects of loyalty. In
less extreme responses, "freedom of conscience" and "conscientious objection" become significant. They are a way of asserting
that some ends shared by others in the society are not acceptable,
or that some socially approved means to ends shared even by the
protestors are objectionable to his personal values. Unless he has
further objections to the society, the citizen permitted exemption
from an obligation on grounds of individual conscience has no
reason to band with others to overthrow social structures or to
accept new and joint obligations.

Despotism suppresses conscientious objectors and those who
demand freedom of conscience as readily as it suppresses revolutionaries. Just as it cannot allow rival institutions or democratic
political parties, it cannot allow personal value as a criterion. One
great difference between democracy and despotism is that democracy accepts the irreducibility of persons, but despotism, particularly in its totalitarian form, attempts to convert all persons to
their social roles, or the sum of their statuses. When persons are
regarded as irreducible, however, many things are allowed them:
eccentricity, personal dissent, pacifism, conscientious objection.
They are bound by the duties that fall on their statuses, to be
sure, but a curious primacy is accorded the person and his values,
especially on appeal to religion or conscience, if it does not result
in serious crime.

Democracy functions chiefly through felt obligation. So
must despotism, as much as it can, but it also indoctrinates rather
than persuades, and if necessary it transforms obligation to command. Fortunately, man is recalcitrant, and many men cling to
their persons and personal judgments even while face to face with
tyranny, and even horror. Whenever despotism relaxes its iron grip,
people behave differently than some social scientists might expect.
They are not, for all that has been done to them, so conditioned
that government can finally dispense with fear and punishment,
hoping without them still to evoke the responses presumably bred
in the people; many of those people promptly demand both a
larger private sphere of action, and genuine participation in
changing their social obligations. Every time the Soviet Union relaxes its oppression, the Sinyavskys and Daniels oppose the government, or demand more relaxation. When Czechoslovakia relaxed its

oppression, Alexander Dubček led a supportive country toward Social Democracy. Some who live under despotisms are broken, of course, but not all; there is still a sense of what it is to be human, which includes freedom, choice, and thought.

I have argued that man's basic choice is whether or not he is to be a moral agent. In qualification, it should be noted that he always is a moral agent, but sometimes with such severe limits that he has little moral agency. Even with a gun in his back a man may refuse to obey, and accept the bullet. But that identifies morality with heroism, and is more than we can expect of most people. To get moral agency for all, we have to choose and if necessary fight for a government that permits freedom and choice, that tolerates or encourages opposition, and that is responsible to its citizens. To have less, I have urged, is to be somewhat—in the extreme, perhaps utterly —dehumanized. And one can see, by comparing democracy and despotism, some of the ways in which despotism dehumanizes.

I have also tried to show some of the strengths of despotism, internal and external, as compared with democracy. But the flexibility of the despotic nation, which I emphasized, is not its only strength; it is also more stable, through its relatively successful attempts to reduce persons to statuses and obligations to commands, and through its ruthless suppression of opposition and dissent—a stability shattered by the relaxation of force. Yet, in non-despotic groups I have posed stability and flexibility against each other, so that usually the greater the one the less the other. Force overcomes that opposition somewhat, by keeping the nation acquiescent in times requiring little change, and by altering obligations without consensus in crisis. In democracy, the stability-flexibility continuum is displayed more fully, and so can be studied better; force, which alters the continuum, is not the normal base of democratic society, and is applied intermittently, mostly in crisis when change is needed and the limits of consensus move in or out. Democracy, too, reveals the other important polarity that affects stability and flexibility: custom and reason, which we will consider at some length.

CHAPTER SEVEN

The Social Functions of the Intellectual

With respect to feelings about the details and ends of group life, men may be placed on an imaginary line, at one extreme of which are those who love the detail and care nothing for the ends, while at the other extreme are those who love the ends but care nothing for the detail, or even dislike it. There may be no such men, but a little way down each end of the line there are several, and there are more and more on each side who are closer to the center. By "detail" I mean the concomitants and trappings of obligation, the emotional tone and ritual of solidarity, the homely or pompous activities that hold men together in work and play. All this cultural furniture is a "way of life."

For brevity, let us call those committed to the detail, "custom-loving men," and those who cherish ends and values, "intellectuals." This is intended to distinguish the men who are bearers of custom from those who are bearers of reason, so that their influence on stability and flexibility can be fleshed. But are there no men who love custom and cherish reason? Of course; yet in decisive moments they must choose one or the other. It is in the choice that they take their places on the imaginary line, and the choice is usually forced on them in crisis. For then new means have to be instituted in order that shared ends can still be realized, and that may bring alteration in lesser ends as well as alteration of obligation, for obligations are means.

Since change in obligation is likely to shatter a way of life, or at least require considerable change in it, one's choice determines whether he is on the custom-loving side of the center or the intellectual side. The intellectual, as I have defined him, is not sheer invention but is, I think, recognizable as a type. He is the heir of the nineteenth-century intelligentsia, and is to be found in many walks of life: student, professor, editor, journalist, writer, artist, musician, lawyer, the young dispossessed, the older upper-middle class. No one of these is made up of intellectuals, but they are the places one is most likely to find them.

Custom-loving men contribute most to the stability of a society, intellectuals to its flexibility. In times of relative stasis, custom-loving men are on the side of group continuance, maintaining its essential character, as well as its way of life, although sometimes they erode group quality by their opposition to small changes, and by their smugness about detail. In times of stasis, the intellectual may injure stability, if he has the power, by deriding custom and proposing constant innovation. In crisis, though, when flexibility is needed, the custom-lover threatens the continuance of the group by his insistence that its detail remain the same, whereas the intellectual supports continuance by sweeping away custom and minor group ends in the interest of new ways of attaining the group's basic ends, thus providing group adaptation to new circumstances. The intellectual is the group's greatest resource in crisis, but to have him when he is needed he must not be crushed when he is not needed.

Much of the flexibility of the intellectual consists in his criticism of existent morality and his proposals for a critical morality. He may not consciously do his job in those terms, but that is the job he does. He may not even like the word "morality," or he may be skeptical about its existence, but his business is morals and standards, and he is a practicing moralist. The intellectual is far more open to change than the custom-loving man: if he is a liberal he tries to widen the limits of consensus, and if he is a conservative he tries to narrow them; if he is sufficiently radical or reactionary, he tries to alter the limits beyond recognition.

A contemporary instance of what I have been saying can be found in several crises that threaten formal education. New ways of teaching, older ways of teaching (e.g., a return to phonetics in learning to read), new subjects, older subjects, new organizations of subject matter, are discussed and introduced. Student bodies, too, are changing; socio-economic levels in which children had little or perfunctory education are now filled with people who demand equal elementary and secondary education, and equal higher education as well. Teachers with few credentials of the traditional sort are being hired for special purposes. The attempt is to save the schools, to continue their main function of education, while changing the means. In the United States, one of the older functions of the schools was to Americanize the children of immigrants, to bring them into the fold in one generation. As the flow of immigrants receded, this function became minor; now it is major again, but with a significant difference. American blacks (that is what they ask to be called) are not immigrants, but they have been kept out of the mainstream of the culture and, so poor and uneducated are their parents relative to white parents, that many of them are ill prepared for work in a good school. The chief difference between American blacks today and white immigrants in the past is that immigrants wanted to be cut to the accepted patterns of American life, but blacks do not; they want to define themselves through links with a black past, and the militants among them want our system to prepare them to overthrow the system.

This difference results in demand for a new kind of socialization and a new kind of education. In the ordinary course of events there might be no serious attempt to meet the demand, but riots, violence, and threats mean either that the schools be barricaded or that they change. Enough past dissatisfaction with the schools from within the schools exists so that some teachers and administrators welcome the chance for change and will try to use the new situation for reform of entirely different kinds. Such behavior is quite predictable, for when the limits of consensus are widened by one crisis (in this case by the pressure of disaffected white and black militants), all kinds of ideas, with insufficient power behind them in the past, are pushed into the breach.

The question asked by committed intellectuals, as always in such crises, is how to preserve the essentials of the group, its major ends, while making the changes that meet the crisis. Since American colleges and universities are not nationally controlled, as in European countries, each school is free to respond to the situation in its own way, and patterns of response may vary widely. This is the time when faculty and administrators will reveal whether they are custom-loving men or intellectuals. The intellectuals' task is what it always is in such cases: choosing new obligations as means to the fundamental and shared ends of the group, finding what must in consequence be discarded, and arguing their various proposals as ably as they can. Even those who save a school from disaster can scarcely hope for popularity, because resistance from the custom-lovers can be predicted, and their academic training will enable many of them to put their cases persuasively.

This educational trauma is not the kind of crisis that shatters civilizations or destroys states; it is the kind that occurs more than once in every life and brings genuine change. In such crises, intellectuals who want to preserve the group because they are devoted to its ends, struggle to find new means that can be accepted. Without the crises, those means would probably be given short shrift by the institution. In crisis, the same means will have a chance of acceptance only if the limits of consensus can be expanded. But custom-loving men, who must be persuaded of the new means, are also enemies of the intellectual who proposes to change or destroy what they hold dear. In the struggle between those who advocate change and those who are determined to prevent it, a new consensus must be forged if the intellectual is to succeed.

Complication is expectable. To begin with, it is unlikely that intellectuals will agree on what must be discarded and what must be initiated. What, in our customary conduct, clogs action or makes group ends unattainable in the new situation? What, in new conduct, would attain those ends under these conditions, and at the same time be economical and efficient? If more than one plausible proposal emerges, intellectuals will quarrel bitterly. Intellectuals may be more divisive than custom-lovers because there are always several ways of resolving practical problems, but there appears to be only one set of customs at any time. That appearance is deceptive because customs of those in different statuses and ranks usually differ, and lovers of custom may love different customs, from those of the wealthy and international to those of the poor who live their lives out in the few square miles—or city blocks—of a ghetto. But intellectuals can be of the same socioeconomic class and still divide sharply on proposals for change; they are more likely to divide into hostile groups than custom-lovers are.

Attack on the intellectuals by custom-lovers can be predicted. In the educational crisis of the moment, custom-lovers and intellectuals will both be found in faculties, school administrations, legislatures, and executive bodies. Bitterness is usually greatest among those closest to each other. Just as most murders take place within families, so custom-lovers and intellectuals within the same subgroups will fight most fiercely. At the same time, they are both under attack by revolutionaries who would destroy the group in its very essence and put something else in its place. From their standpoint, the intellectual committed to the group is far from the friend he thinks he is; he thinks indeed that he is serving the revolutionaries' needs by his proposals, and expects to be welcomed. Yet he is saving the group the revolutionaries want to destroy. If he is more likely to save it than the custom-lover is, he is the greater enemy in the eyes of the revolutionary.

To some student militants the schools should be training grounds for those who will overthrow the larger society and replace it with something better. In extreme cases, militants have asked for courses in guerrilla warfare. They demand a new "education" so they can learn, first, to grasp the levers of power and use them for efficient destruction of hated institutions and values. Then, second, they must learn how to construct new institutions, create new values, and manipulate what results to the ends they share.

The new "education" is not education at all to nonrevolutionaries, whether custom-lovers or intellectuals. They are committed to older traditions, in which preparation for a single social role or function might be vocational training but could never be education. And this particular vocational training is absurd to them because one cannot ask the society that supports the schools to subsidize its own destruction.

In crisis, then, the intellectual devoted to group ends is embattled against the custom-lovers who prefer group means and also against the perennial revolutionaries who oppose both the ends and the means. A third army of enemies will be other intellectuals with quite different proposals. If it seems that intellectuals at such times could easily resolve their differences by rational discourse, or that they could always ally themselves with custom-lovers against revolutionaries, the underlying problem has been missed. The problem lies in the relation of means to ends. Except in very simple cases, where differences are negligible, one cannot use different means to yield exactly the same end.

If I decide to buy a newspaper, and am almost equally distant from two newsstands, my decision to go to one or the other does not alter the end in any significant way. Whichever of the two directions I take, I get the newspaper. It is not the identical paper, but it is the same paper in having identical content; it contains the same information, which is what I want. I may get |the paper a bit earlier or later, but that probably does not matter. For practical purposes, the same end could be obtained by different means. In more complex cases, though, this is rarely the case.

Changes in subject matter, curriculum, teaching methods, ratio of faculty to students, proportion of faculty time devoted to teaching and to research, criteria of student admission, systems of grading, and requirements for a degree would change the kind and quality of university education. One can only talk of different means to the same end if the end is quite general, and not precisely specified. So an educated man or woman can be produced by quite different means, if our criteria of education are general enough—a well skilled and a well-stocked mind, for instance. Indeed, mediocre schools turn out some highly educated graduates if the library has a few books and there are one or two people to talk to.

The intellectual is always proposing, in crisis, not just a change in obligatory means but, at least implicitly, some alteration in shared ends. Education, after changes in the organization of schools, is not quite the same education it was before, for example. So the intellectual cannot so easily resolve differences in his own ranks; different proposals for change in means become proposals for some alteration in ends. New questions have to be asked about the extent to which the altered ends realize the same values the earlier ends did, and about the willingness to agree on the new ends, to share them. Intellectuals may be irreconcilable on these matters. And custom-loving men become aware that altered ends will, in turn, further alter customary surroundings. If products of a new education, for instance, differ sufficiently from products of the older education, we will be faced with a new generation of college graduates unlike the past generation. And that can be more serious than it sounds, for the new generation will claim its place

in the ranks of the educated, and will perhaps transform the ordinary conditions of their lives.

One virtue of this complex process of somewhat deliberate
change is that all manner of questions are asked that are unlikely
to surface in authoritarian groups. Reason is employed in a fuller
sense, and solutions are likely to provide for better adaptation and
adjustment to new conditions than authoritarian groups will ever
get. The intellectual plays a decisive part in resolving crisis, and
may have greater prestige and recognition than is his lot at other
times, although he has a continuing function then, too.

Even when there is no crisis, providing flexibility involves
offering alternatives as ways of attaining shared ends, examining
and criticizing those ends and the values from which they come,
perhaps proposing changes in them, and appraising all the concomitants of obligation, the entire way of life. The intellectual
also performs the function of examining and enunciating values
neglected in the culture, and values alternative to those of the
culture. Then he has his own class values, those of the intellectual
class, truth, excellence, and beauty, and he maintains these, when
he is at his best, against the values of the dominant economic
class, and against the values of the economic market. Whatever
ability the intellectual has to resist the conditioning of his fellow
citizens probably comes from his habituation to thought and the
company of his peers, which bring some detachment from the
immediate and the material.

The personal characteristics of today's intellectual and his
position in society need examination so we can understand what
he is and how likely he is to perform his functions. Those very
functions have led intellectuals in the past to a nagging unhappi-
ness with their condition: if anyone knows enough to rule, they
think, it is they. Underlying their overt political preferences is
perhaps a special feeling for Plato's intellectual aristocracy. This is
not a living option, but it may be a secret allegiance.

Some intellectuals too easily deprecate the other qualities it
takes to lead and rule, besides mind and imagination. Those include hardiness, reliability, quick and accurate calculation of risk,
self-assurance, and administrative ability. Many of these qualities
are outside the intellectual's training, and he may value them too
little. He may also deprecate people who possess them, because

they are rewarded by our society for traits that are seldom his. American intellectuals rarely attain the status of their European counterparts in some countries, and that is often a source of complaint, although it is less a higher European regard for intellectuals that is at issue than a more elaborate rank structure in Europe, with perhaps greater deference for all high statuses.

In a middle-class world, businessman and intellectual mingle little and are too often suspicious of each other. The division between them, sometimes honored in the breach, is at bottom a tendency of businessmen to judge the worth of men and products in market terms of what they will bring materially, while the intellectual, ideally, uses his own standards of excellence. (Only ideally. The academic intellectual is greatly influenced by the academic market place, and too readily judges colleagues by the demand for them and the salaries they get.) The difference is that of the intellectual's trained and educated judgment versus the judgment of the population as a whole. The latter, recorded in price and sales, is accepted as correct by the businessman but not by the intellectual; yet the intellectual is paid by the standards of the market, not by his own, unlike the businessman, whose pay is determined by his own standards, which are those of the market.

To expand these differences is to reveal the relation of the intellectual to middle-class culture. Since, for the businessman, ideally, making products for sale and purchase, or simply buying and selling what others have made, is central to his life and thought, he treats values in quasi-economic terms.

1. Products are judged by the demand for them, especially effective demand, which is backed by money. Thus the businessman's taste and judgment are not his own, but the taste and judgment of the market.

2. Actions are undertaken if they are presumed to yield profit, in any of its senses: money, advancement, or prestige. Thus actions are not performed because of internal or intrinsic judgment, nor as means to psychic satisfactions or self-development, but for their external consequences.

3. Plans are judged by their economy, efficiency, and ultimate profitability. Thus there is only secondary concern with their consequences for human life and human environment. (Think of the growing pollution of the earth and business resistance to proposals for additional business expenditure to control it or for more government controls.)

4. The value of a person or thing is expressible (and expressed) in monetary terms. Thus the value set on a man is largely determined by the amount of money he makes.

For the intellectual, again ideally, the life of mind and the quest for excellence are central, and other values reflect these.

1. An intellectual or artistic work is true, excellent, revealing, stimulating, or it is not approved. Thus intellectual or artistic work is judged by the criteria of the judge, not by the momentary taste of the majority as expressed in the market.

2. Actions are undertaken if they seem interesting or important. Thus to undertake action purely for the sake of profit is a denial of the intellectual's major values. (Of course, that is often necessary, in actual cases, but it is not as intellectual that a man does it, although his intellectual abilities and his knowledge may be what he sells. And too many intellectuals are corrupted by news media, the academy, and other institutions, into work they find uninteresting and trivial, but rewarding in pay, rank, and prestige.)

3. Plans are sometimes judged by their economy and efficiency in yielding intellectual or artistic ends, sometimes in moral, hedonist (e.g., boring or exciting), or aesthetic terms. Thus external consequence is subordinated to the possible quality of the product and its psychic effects.

4. The value of a person or thing is expressible as talent, merit, beauty, excellence, potential, and accomplishment. Thus reward, prestige, and their concomitants are regarded as adventitious, not essential. (This is important for the description of the intellectual ideal that attracts many young people. In practice, it is incredibly rare, and requires self-sacrifice; it exists a little more among genuine intellectuals than among the technicians who pass themselves off as intellectuals.)

The intellectual and the businessman, as ideal types, are opposed in our civilization, but even the ideal businessman is not entirely the custom-loving man of our earlier antithesis. And intellectuals, except in times of crisis, are themselves often custom-loving, and may even try to convert custom into a principle of civilization. They do not then mean by custom the ways of the moment, but rather the best ways of the past and the amenities of life at their most civilized. These intellectuals are aware that manners as well as morals are important, because they serve morality.

They do so by relating people to each other in a manner that minimizes friction and represses hostility, while it provides occasion and incentives to cooperation. Manners, of course, add immeasurably to the charms of life. Yet they are opposed by other intellectuals as artificial, and repressive of natural expression. Undoubtedly, manners sometimes are so formal as to be repressive, and so elaborate as to border on the ridiculous. But opposition to manners does not breed non-manners, only other manners. We do not know what it would mean to be "natural," even in the bedroom (itself "artificial" for its purposes), because we are as social as we are natural. Codes of manners are to be judged by what they add to life, and especially, in the end, by how they serve morality.

The businessman, as an ideal type, stands for change, but only change in the direction of maximized profit and self-aggrandizement, and even then perhaps just for the moment, because it takes discipline to give up a bird in the hand for a possible two in the bush. The businessman's values have accorded with, and supported, both science and democratic government, by their emphasis on rational decision and individualism. But when custom interferes with profit, custom is denounced as retarding progress which, in business ideology, is a result of the unrestrained pursuit of profit. So nationally protected forests go for lumber, beaches for recreation become oil wells, and water and air are polluted so industrial wastes can be disposed of cheaply.

Despite all this, the businessman is today, as he was not at the beginning of the bourgeois revolutions, a great defender of custom. He enjoys the pleasurable customs of the time and, if he spoils one beach for the sake of oil, he can afford to vacation at another. The prestige and perquisites of wealth are his, and he fears a basic dislocation of custom and convention. Above all, despite the tension between existent custom and business "advances," he knows that the folkways of business are deeply imbedded in custom. What this amounts to is that custom is not a solid rock; it has cracks in it and divisions, some of it is loved by some people, and some by others. But in crisis, the test of whether we stand with reason or with custom is whether or not we will alter or forego *our* custom to preserve the values we share. Another way of stating the test is to ask which we value more highly, our own beloved customs or our cherished goals.

To leave the ideal, the image we make for ourselves and sometimes hide behind as a mask, there are some of the qualities of the intellectual in the businessman and many of the qualities of the businessman in the intellectual. Not that there are no nearly pure examples of each, but that the intellectual ideal, like the ideal of the saint or philosopher, touches multitudes, while the ethos of a business society permeates most breasts. Many people of inherited wealth, and rich members of what is called the "Eastern Establishment" in the United States, forego profit for public service and demand change to overcome poverty and inequality. Official intellectuals, like university professors, few of whom are more than technical experts—and sometimes poor ones—scramble so for advancement, prestige, and money that there is often little to choose in this respect between universities and the giant business corporations they come more and more to resemble.

One point often made in favor of university faculties is that there is more money to be made in business than in the academy, and while many academicians are bright enough to succeed in business, they chose the academy instead. That point loses much of its force when it becomes clear that many of the brightest academicians lack qualities needed in business, cannot tolerate a nine-to-five working day, or cannot stand overt and acknowledged competition. Others of the greatest ability chose academic life when they were young and conceived it in the ideal garb with which it clothes itself; disillusioned now, they think it too late to start a new career. Then, of course, there are some of many talents who are intellectuals, could succeed in many pursuits including business, know the failings of the academy and its limitation of their income, and still choose it as a way of life.

For all this mixture of business and intellectual traits in many men, there remains a distinction between the two, both ideally and in practice. Of course, some professors, editors, novelists, and painters are businessmen at heart and in much of their behavior. Of course, some businessmen are intellectuals. But those who are at bottom businessmen are custom-lovers, and those who are at bottom intellectuals stand for change when need be. The same distinction is found among laborers, government employees, presidents and prime ministers.

One way in which this bears on morality, beyond what has

been said about it so far, is that conventional morality is part, even a great part, of cultural detail. Whatever the personal morality of the custom-lover or intellectual, there is a stance toward morals in times of relative stability that is intensified in crisis. The custom-lover is moralistic, insisting upon the ancient virtues. One hears the typical businessman condemning the faintest deviations from the norm, even confusing unconventional garb with immorality, while he himself may be engaged in price-fixing, suborning justice, and much else that is shabby as well as immoral. The intellectual is dubious of conventional pieties, and makes more individual judgments about moral conduct than the businessman. The issue, in or out of crisis, is conventional versus critical morality, the love of the existent and the fear of change versus the love of the ideal, or at least the choice of what seems, on reflection, the better. Unless crisis is great enough to bring our values themselves into question, the issue is between customary obligations and goals or ends.

When crisis does bring our values into question, a third type becomes important, the revolutionist. He is outside the stability-flexibility continuum because he does not choose between customs and goals; he rejects both. He may or may not reject the basic values of the group; indeed, he may maintain that only he can realize them. Inside a revolutionary organization, he may become a lover of its customs or an intellectual who sometimes opposes current revolutionary obligations and other customs in order to further the revolution itself. Revolutionary organizations are groups, too, and within them are stability-flexibility continua of their own; on those continua each revolutionist has his place, determined by his devotion to custom or reason. But in the outside groups he wants to "overthrow," he stands neither for custom or reason (he may think of himself as representing a larger reasonableness), but as destroyer of group means, ends, and most customs. Unless he is a lone and ineffective revolutionist, he plays two roles, one within a revolutionary group and one outside a revolutionary group.

We are now implicitly defining the revolutionary as one who rejects the shared ends of a group or nation (depending on his scope) and so rejects the obligations that are supposed to yield them. The ends we share are based on our values or advantages, and on situations in which *these* ends, rather than others, are chosen to realize our values. All revolutionists are, I think, as I defined them: men who reject the shared ends of groups in which they have membership so that, in crisis, they would not try to attain the ends by other means, but would prefer that the group lose its essential quality of shared ends. Although the revolutionist, too, may be an intellectual, he is one who does not perform the intellectual's basic function in society. In writing of that function I have assumed consent to, or acquiescence in, membership—with all that implies—and the revolutionist does not give his consent.

With respect to how much he rejects of his own nonrevolutionary group or society, the revolutionist may be in either of two orders (no ranking or value preference is intended, just a distinction): those who reject the shared ends but accept the values; and those who reject both the ends and the values, and more surely the values than the ends. In the first order are revolutionists who argue, perhaps implicitly, that the ends of the group betray the group's values, perhaps because the situation in which the ends were chosen is long past or perhaps because the ends are as ill-suited to the values as obligations often are to ends. If purity of spirit in the love of God is a value, and celibacy is one end chosen to help realize it (celibacy is not a means in the sense that being celibate makes one pure in spirit; it may make one a rapist), then monastic life with all its obligations is a means to help attain celibacy, among other ends. In the language I am using, one attains an end but realizes a value.

A monastic reformer may want to change his obligations because they do not attain their ends. In the matter of celibacy, monastic life of a certain kind may provide monks with sexual access to nuns or peasant girls, and sexual fantasies heated by certain devotions and texts may make it difficult to exercise restraint. A monastic revolutionary of the first order will oppose celibacy, denying that it helps realize spiritual purity. And a monastic revolutionary of the second order might not only oppose celibacy, which to him may or may not be one realization of spiritual purity, but will oppose spiritual purity itself. Indeed, if this revolutionary believes that celibacy defeats purity, he may defend celibacy and reject other ends which do seem to him to be realizations of purity. The history of medieval heresy reveals stranger things.

Karl Marx was a revolutionary of the first order and so, to some extent, was Lenin, who may have been in both orders, but Adolf Hitler was clearly of the second order, as perhaps was Robespierre. One great difference between 1776 and 1789, I think, is that American revolutionists were, for the most part, either in the first order or in neither, being social reformers fighting for national independence, while French revolutionists were partly in the second order, denying the values of the *ancien régime* though defending reason and some Judeo-Christian morality. The greater stability of the American Republic may reflect just this difference, for the American Revolution, waged in an English intellectual context, appealed in the Declaration of Independence to the values and ends of the Enlightenment and used, as Jefferson said, the ideas of Aristotle, Cicero, Sidney, and Locke. The French context was less liberal than the English, and the underlying appeal of the French revolutionists was to Platonic and Cartesian Reason, with the Rousseauean addition of the General Will, in which all rational men agreed.

As for Marx, he is a genuine case of the intellectual revolutionist of the first order: his value-base could be summarized as agreement with the major values of Judeo-Christian tradition, plus insistence that the means and ends of bourgeois society realized antithetical values, antithetical even to the avowed values of capitalism as enunciated by Adam Smith and others. Only through the social revolution and the socialism that followed, he thought, could the great values of capitalism be realized: freedom, equality, opportunity, and reward for individual merit. And only through eventual communism could the values of Christianity be realized: concern for others unimpeded by self-seeking, release from purely material considerations, treatment of each according to his needs. Marx proposed new ends to realize the values he held, and new social structures to yield those ends. If he was not clear about the obligations necessary for his ends, he was open to whatever obligations would develop. Russia was his posthumous Waterloo.

Hitler is a prime example of a revolutionist of the second order, and not an intellectual at all, in the sense Marx was. Of course, he continued many things in the German tradition, especially the military tradition, which could have been derived just as easily from nations like France, but no one can start everything afresh. Hitler's main ideological thrust was what Aurel Kolnai called "the war against the west," which involved utter repudiation of the Judeo-Christian tradition, and so of an entire civilization. His values were forged in opposition to Christian values, whether in religious or secularized form. The greatest puzzle about his policy is his insistence on carrying antisemitism to the "final solution," even when that was not just ruthless efficiency or national advantage, but a danger to his success in war, through a use of materials, money, time, and manpower that could ill be spared. Let me speculate about it.

A war against the west is a war against Christendom, in all its religious and irreligious forms. But even for Hitler, it was hopeless to try to meet Christianity head on, in avowed combat. Hitler accepted, I think, Nietzsche's perverted notion of the origin of Christianity in *The Antichrist,* while rejecting Nietzsche's high evaluation (with qualifications) of the Jew. Nietzsche's thesis, in brief, is that a tiny nation, defeated by Pompey and kept in subjugation to the vast Roman Empire, tried direct revolt unsuccessfully, again and again, and finally deliberately created an ideological revolution that would bring it not just freedom but conquest, first of Rome and then of the western world. That revolution was Christianity, which destroyed the virtues of the warrior and substituted those of the slave, so that the new communicants would never themselves revolt. Hitler even followed Nietzsche in believing that Jesus had not intended the use the Jews made of his teachings, and that Paul (as so many intellectuals of the late nineteenth century thought) was the villain of the piece.

The Nietzschean thesis was seen by Hitler through the glass of his own antisemitic mania:

> The decisive falsification of Jesus' doctrine was the work of St. Paul . . . . For the Galilean's object was to liberate His country from Jewish expression. He set Himself against Jewish capitalism, and that's why the Jews liquidated Him.
>
> Paul of Tarsus (his name was Saul before the road to Damascus) was one of those who persecuted Jesus most savagely. When he learnt that Jesus' supporters let their throats be cut for His ideas, he realized that, by making intelligent use of the Galilean's teaching, it would be possible to overthrow this Roman state which the Jews hated. It's in this

context that we must understand the famous "illumination." Think of it, the Romans were daring to confiscate the most sacred thing that the Jews possessed, the gold piled up in their temples! At that time, as now, money was their god.

On the road to Damascus, St. Paul discovered that he could succeed in ruining the Roman state by causing the principle to triumph of the equality of all men before a single God—and by putting beyond the reach of the laws his private notions, which he alleged to be divinely inspired. If, into the bargain, one succeeded in imposing one man as the representative on earth of the only God, that man would possess boundless power.*

In his own peculiar way, Hitler understood that Marxism, although "materialistic" and anti-religious, accepted many Christian values. For that alone he hated it. "Christianity is a prototype of Bolshevism: the mobilization by the Jew of the masses of slaves with the object of undermining society."** Putting these ideas together, Hitler said:

The heaviest blow that ever struck humanity was the coming of Christianity. Bolshevism is Christianity's illegitimate child. Both are inventions of the Jew. The deliberate lie in the matter of religion was introduced into the world by Christianity. Bolshevism practices a lie of the same nature, when it claims to bring liberty to men, whereas in reality it seeks only to enslave them. In the ancient world, the relations between men and gods were founded on an instinctive respect. It was a world enlightened by the idea of tolerance. Christianity was the first creed in the world to exterminate its adversaries in the name of love. Its keynote is intolerance.†

The tolerant Hitler had an extraordinary scheme for eliminating Christianity: he would get Christians to kill Jews. At one stroke, the fountainhead of Christianity would disappear, and

---

*Hitler's Secret Conversations, 1941-1944, Farrar, Straus, and Young, 1953, p. 63

**Ibid., p. 62.

†Ibid., p. 6.

every Christian involved in the killing would have compromised his Christianity. Hitler would thus have destroyed the values he inherited, and would be free to replace them. He had, of course, little to replace them with: tawdry dreams of a Teutonic past, peopled with Wagnerian operatic gods, German heroes and conquerors, and the trappings of power. The successful revolutionist of the second order must persuade people of a new gospel, complete with a new set of values, for he does not have traditional beliefs and values to appeal to; he must shatter the limits of consensus and create new ones. He must not only know what he opposes, and why, but what he proposes in its place. Jesus was such a successful revolutionary; there were not very many others.

I have said that Marx was an intellectual and Hitler was not. When revolutions are based on theories and proposals, they have an intellectual founder; when they are based on dissatisfaction and hatred, and offer only vague promises for the future, intellectuals function in them only as publicists and expositors. The American, the French, and the Russian revolutions had remarkable intellectual forerunners and participants. The fascist revolutions in Italy, Spain, and Portugal were carried out in the face of opposition by famous intellectuals (Croce and Ortega, to name but two of many) but had few intellectuals of repute who aided the cause (Gentile, in Italy, was perhaps the ablest). The Nazi revolution had some intellectual forerunners, but had few participants or apologists of distinction (Heidegger and Jung were perhaps the most famous). For theoretical justification, the Nazis had to rely on intellectual journalists like Alfred Rosenberg.

The evidence to date more or less supports the generalization that when intellectuals make up a good deal of the leadership of a revolution, they are destroyed within a generation or two, as in the French and Russian revolutions, and are replaced by minor ideologists, advertising men, and publicists, who defend and promote the new regime and its leaders on order. The new leadership is made up of bureaucrats, who give the orders to intellectuals. Even in the American Revolution, the philosophical statesmen who provided its ideas were slowly replaced by soldiers, bureaucrats, and businessmen. The line of aristocratic, scholarly republicans who were presidents ended with John Quincy Adams; Andrew Jackson was a new type and provided a new ideal, the man of the people.

Although they do not prosper long after a successful revolution, revolution itself often has an attraction to intellectuals, who are usually too little rewarded, are often impatient with a world they criticize, and are prepared with less pain than others to junk their cultural furniture in the interest of their goals. Communism held a fascination for many intellectuals, and still does for a few, because of the humane values of Marxism, its scientific pretensions, and its presumed path to Utopia. When it became clear that Communism as practiced was tyranny, most western intellectuals gave it up. Some were compromised and could not leave; some were intimidated; some sold out for rewards no one else would offer. It is unfortunately easy for a man with the skills but not the character of an intellectual to betray his cause, especially when his roots are not deep in the common soil of custom and habit, and he may acquire the businessman's trait of offering everything he has for sale. When he becomes a publicist, for ideas or commodities, the intellectual perverts his function, sells only the least of his abilities, and represses what is basic to the intellectual enterprise, criticism and new hypothesis.

When he is not tempted by revolution the intellectual is more likely to be attracted to liberalism than conservatism, partly for its current concern with the poor, the disinherited, and the future, but chiefly because the heart of liberalism is a belief in the value and importance of the individual act of thought. That belief has been central to liberalism, historically, and it is a necessary assumption, because liberalism stands for deliberate, beneficial change, and such change requires knowledge of a situation, proposals for action, and tests to find whether the action attains its ends. That is, in effect, the intellectual's function as I have described it, and it gives scope to his talents. The intellectual is a man of ideas; if he enters a liberal political group and prospers in it, his ideas may cease to be merely private, and find a practical embodiment.

Conservatism attracts intellectuals less than liberalism does, but has a genuine attraction nonetheless. Conservatism seems to play (but really does not) against the intellectual's social role by making custom-lovers the bearers of both the tradition and progress. But that has its own charms. Intellectuals, like any minority that suffers discrimination and antipathy, have a talent for self-hatred, often revealed in dreams of glory. By siding with the custom-lover, they implicitly deride other intellectuals but exonerate themselves, as blacks sometimes do in defending whites, or Jews in defending Christians. The self-hatred is thus projected onto others of the same class, and one is both in it and above it. Further, intellectuals who become conservatives have special individuality, because their political position distinguishes them from other intellectuals, and they have a quality of shock in the intellectual world: they say startling things, startling because of the paradox that they say them, and, of course, say them better than other conservatives.

There are genuine intellectuals who are genuine conservatives as well, including many of those I have just described. Conservatism does not, as I just said, really play against the intellectual's social role, especially when a generally liberal attitude predominates and is fostered by what Sidney Hook has called ritualistic liberals, those for whom liberalism is an unthinking creed to be applied mechanically to every new social and moral problem. In this situation ritualistic liberals determine the limits of consensus that presumably apply to intellectuals. For those whose function in society is to provide flexibility, limits are imposed by others, supposedly among them, who insist that flexibility be rigid, that alternatives to what exists can only be of one kind. In dealing with poverty or education, for example, the ritualistic liberal condemns any intellectual who thinks the problem cannot be solved by massive government aid. This allows the conservative intellectual to make proposals that would widen the limits of consensus and yet not offend conservative sentiment. Thus the conservative intellectual performs the intellectual's function of offering new alternatives (even if some are old but no longer used) and stepping into the breach of crisis.

There is a vast difference between conservative intellectuals and habit-ridden conservatives, so prominent in business and government, just as there is between liberal intellectuals and ritualistic liberals. Even in a generally conservative society, the conservative intellectual defends the ends and values of the society but will offer, chiefly in crisis, new means to attain the ends (and so new obligations) and sometimes new ends to realize basic conservative values. As intellectual, he is more devoted to conservative values than to ends, and to ends more than means. He can be prolific in proposing new means, as witness the conservative economist Milton Friedman. But he may still remain an object of suspicion to liberal intellectuals, who assume too easily that no conservative can be an intellectual because all conservatives, by definition, defend the status quo. What is overlooked, of course, is that the status quo may be conventional means, or obligations, defended unthinkingly by habit-ridden conservatives, who are lovers of custom, or they may be ends and values, defended by conservative intellectuals.

Some nations treat intellectuals quite well, and are repaid in prestige and stability. The danger in treating intellectuals badly is that they can create more dissatisfaction than any other class: it is in the national interest to treat them well. The United States, with a history of recent anti-intellectualism, and considerable radical ferment among intellectuals in the 1930s, is doing well in this respect, although not deliberately, because the intellectual— including the poet, painter, and musician—has been able to find a home in the academy and to partake of the relatively high prestige of the professor. In addition, faculty salaries have risen and professors can now live like comfortable members of the lower or middle-middle class.

When intellectuals are kept out of the establishment and regarded as cranks, their articulateness alone makes them dangerous to stability. They usually know they are too few and too weak to have a genuine power base of their own. So, in seeking their own power, they tend to ally with a larger class, and become its spokesmen, as they did with the bourgeoisie in the eighteenth century, and the bourgeoisie and the proletariat in turn in the nineteenth and early twentieth centuries. When they want power individually within the status quo, some intellectuals can move into big business, especially entertainment and news media. It is even possible for intellectuals to join the New Conservatism today and so affiliate, at least psychically, with an aristocracy or a caste. The earlier intellectual conservatives in twentieth=century America were often southerners who returned to older values of family and manners; at their best, they played the part of aristocrats properly: they accepted responsibility for standards and taste without demanding reward.

The intellectual searches for stability in his own life as every-one does. That search takes interesting forms, partly because the intellectual is ingenious, partly because he is an avatar of flexi-bility, to whom the ordinary stability of the custom-lover may be strange. There is even guilt in being on the side of flexibility, for one may someday be forced to destroy the parental home in order to build a better one. Personal stability for the intellectual cannot be found in society as he knows it, if he is constantly advocating changes in it, but some intellectuals find it in the eternal, which never changes, whether the eternal be heaven or mathematics. Bertrand Russell, in *A Free Man's Worship,* made a case for the Platonic realm of essence as the intellectual's proper habitation; and "Cyrenaics" like Walter Pater found that permanent concentra-tion on temporary pleasures would yield something like the eter-nal, or so they said. The obvious place to find the eternal has not been neglected, and there have been many religious conversions, or returns to family religion, among twentieth-century intellectuals.

Intellectuals may of course dream of stable societies in the future to which they give their allegiance now, sometimes fore-saking allegiance to their homelands. That is fairly common at the moment of this writing, although the outline of that future is dim. The generation or two so influenced by T. S. Eliot looked to stable societies of the past to give shape to the present; the inter-est of many was medieval and they made a cult of Dante. That has not survived so well as another way to stability taken by Eliot and Joyce and others, philosophers and psychologists as well as poets. Recurrence was the key, and it was found in myth, not in a type of myth but in recurrence of the same mythical themes in religion, the psyche, language, and art. Stability of the human psyche was thus provided beyond the instabilities of groups and societies. Perhaps the latest move of intellectuals to ally themselves with something stable is ordinary language philosophy, in which philosophical meanings are derived from the use of words in ordi-nary language. Like most of the earlier moves, this is conservative, for it presupposes that wisdom is embodied in something very like a continuing institution, the old and standard expression of cus-tom-loving men.

Some nations, like France and an older Germany, bound intellectuals to them by making a place for them, and a high one, in the hierarchy of society. Totalitarian nations, especially those that are communist, are careful to accord intellectuals whatever is needed to keep them loyal, except what intellectuals need most, which is freedom. The history of totalitarianism betrays its need for ideologists and publicists, and the initial revolutionary success of totalitarianism shows how dangerous dissatisfied intellectuals can be to the status quo. To keep intellectuals in and of the group, and perhaps to tempt them to sell their birthright, at least five things must be done for them. First, there is moral reinforcement: they must be told they do good and are valuable to the society. Second, they must be paid well, for apart from its obvious value, that shows how highly they are regarded. Third, they must have—or seem to have—prestige in the seats of the mighty. An occasional dinner at the White House, the Kremlin, or Downing Street helps greatly. Fourth, they must be offered the chance of general reputation with the public, for the intellectual usually wants to be more than caviare to the general.

The fifth inducement to the intellectual is fame. Secret ambition gnaws at many intellectuals; they desire fame, but dare not admit it, because then they do not have to admit failure, too, but can pretend to a maturity that thinks fame a bauble. Youth is taught its heroes well and every composer wants to be a new Bach, every painter a new Rembrandt, every novelist a new Tolstoy. With years, and perhaps indolence, great ambition is banked, but it needs only the breeze of possibility to fan a new flame. The frustration of high ambition is commonplace: how many names are on all lips, like Newton's or Kant's; but the frustration is a secret sorrow. How fortunate are those who learn a new way to fame—immortality, to the young—without needing the talents of a Shakespeare or Leonardo. And there is such a way. It has existed for a long time, but today it can be bartered for loyalty. It is simply that the state says you are great, and people must accept its judgments. Show loyalty to a tyrannical state and you will be exalted above those with greater talents but less loyalty.

Nations and other groups, even families, have their great men, but only on the national level is a great man truly great. When a nation does not produce a man of as great accomplishment as its neighbors' heroes, it still chooses the best it has, and tries to give him world fame. That is a matter of national pride, and feeds patriotism, so it is a serious concern of every nation. All avenues to greatness are opened: heroism, martyrdom, statesmanship, philanthropy, art, philosophy, science; and each has its ennobled figure. America has Nathan Hale, Switzerland has William Tell, the Third Reich had Horst Wessel, and they serve the same purpose. Small nations, and new ones, may make do with second-best, and pretend they are more. How else account for the national reputations of Jean Sibelius and César Franck?

But totalitarianism can quite deliberately support the reputations of the second-best and the genuinely mediocre with all the power of a national press and party-line criticism. In a lesser way, totalitarian parties in democratic nations can offer a highly organized apparatus to create and maintain reputations. When the Communist Party of the United States was at its height, America's most touted novelists were not just Faulkner and Hemingway and Fitzgerald, whose reputations the Party could not destroy, but Albert Maltz and Howard Fast. The Soviet Union has its social realist painters, East Germany treated Bertolt Brecht as though he were Shakespeare—Shakespeare, alas, was not treated as though he was Shakespeare—and Lysenko, for a time, was another Darwin.

Knowing the intellectual's needs, his natural enemies know his price; sometimes he has one. If he can be bought, the intellectual ceases to be genuine and turns his talents to the defense of stability. With the whole power of the state protecting stability, and few offering flexibility—if an intellectual cannot be bought, he can be destroyed—totalitarian nations resist change as democratic nations do not, and can throttle internal crises in their infancy. And when crisis comes, the state can meet it quickly and often efficiently, for it need not be concerned with the limits of consensus where consensus is helpless and force provides power. The temporary thaw in Czechoslovak repression was largely the work of intellectuals. But they were powerless against Soviet tanks.

Here, though, is the fundamental weakness of the totalitarian structure. What alternatives are considered to meet crisis, and who proposes them? How much imagination goes into proposing new means which can yield group ends in new situations? How much reflection and discussion precede decision? The emasculated intellectuals of totalitarianism cannot be counted on, nor is the public allowed to participate. The job is done by ruling bureaucrats, who have neither the training for it nor the natural abilities. When Czechoslovakia's move toward democratic socialism was crushed, bureaucrats like Husak took charge of the new sovietization and intellectuals were repressed. When crisis is more than bureaucrats can handle, the society will collapse or turn peacefully to freedom.

The strength of a democratic government in crisis lies in wealth of alternatives and independence of judgment. The weakness of despotism is that alternatives are fewer, and probably less good and judgment is not made with the fierce independence that should characterize the intellectual. Speed of decision is a specialty of despotism, but democracy's disadvantage in that respect may be minimized by forethought and preparation for possible crisis. Although consensus must be attained in democracy, and the limits of consensus widened, there is an opportunity for discussion, new points of view, and popular support. Despotism has the intelligence and articulateness of intellectuals at its disposal, even though they no longer have the full character of intellectuals. The problem of democracy in this respect is to support genuine intellectuals and affirm intellectual values when there is no crisis, so intellectuals will be ready, and loyal, when crisis comes.

CHAPTER EIGHT

Society, Politics, and Function

Since one cannot deal with morality profitably without also dealing with the social and political activities of man, I shall take this occasion to inquire into them. Of necessity I shall say some things about the academic subjects in which they are studied, but I have neither the ability nor the inclination to persuade sociologists and political scientists to do work of one kind rather than another. They do what the past growth and current state of their disciplines make rewarding, and a new analysis is not likely to affect the directions they take. But social philosophy requires a new analysis, I think, and is entitled to view the studies men make as well as the actions they perform. I shall start with the studies, in the manner of one who does not himself make them, as a way of getting to what, ideally if not actually, I take to be their subjects.

Society and politics are staples of everyday conversation and subjects of learned treatises, but what are they and how are they related? Since I shall try to answer these questions in terms derived from the concept of social function it would be neither fair nor wise to neglect so important a body of social theory as functionalism. So I shall deal with what is relevant in functionalism briefly and critically as a way of getting to a new starting place. But first, a word about sociology is in order, for it is there that the largest body of functional theory exists.

As one looks at work in sociology, he finds that part of the subject are the relations among activities and institutions that are studied *per se* in other subjects. Relations of education and the family, economics and social classes, government and art, science and philanthropy, are regular examples of sociological study. Another part of sociology is just as evident: behavior that is in the interstices of other studies, or that has a sociological dimension, i.e., is related to activities that do not fall within the rubric of the study that might be expected normally to contain it. Thus suicide, as Durkheim has shown once and for all, is not entirely a psychological matter. If we ask under what political, economic, familial, and educational conditions suicide occurs, and in what amount, that is a sociological question, just as it is a philosophical and moral question if we ask whether suicide is justified under any conditions and, if so, which ones.

The focus of most subjects is such that some things, even important ones, are left over; they may be regarded for a time as no more than the crumbs dropped from a scientific table, but put together they sometimes turn out to be a full meal. Just so, political studies of the formal structure of governmental agencies, Congress, or the United Nations may leave out all considerations of informal organization, and these may then be the content of serious research in sociology.

But is there more? In addition to the overview of society, the connections of its parts, and the matters ruled out of other subjects by their very definitions or momentary concerns, is there also a special matter that makes up, or defines, the specifically sociological? I think so, and I think that subject matter can be found by examining the concept of function.

In sociology, as in anthropology, function has for years been distinguished from structure, in much the way physiology has from anatomy, although to avoid a seeming neglect of structure in the functional analysis of society, some sociologists speak of that analysis as a "structural-functional" approach. The idea of "functionalism" may be borrowed from physiology, but except for the concerñ in both cases with survival and organization, functionalism in sociology has only a few similarities to functionalism in physiology. (Manifest functions cannot be found in biology at all.) Yet, however it is derived, it is fairly clear what is meant by "function" in sociology today.

A. R. Radcliffe-Brown defined social function in 1935 (elaborating an idea Durkheim had stated in 1895) in a way still generally acceptable: "The function of any recurrent activity . . . is the part it plays in the social life as a whole and therefore the contribution it makes to the maintenance of the structural continuity."* More recently, heavy emphasis has been placed on the "contribution" to the maintenance of "social systems." A phenomenon is said to be functional for a system, or more simply, "functional," if its effects adjust or adapt elements in the system; it is said to be "dysfunctional" if its effects decrease the adjustment or adaptation of elements in the system; and it is called "nonfunctional" if it does not affect the system at all. It should be noted that the nonfunctional (sometimes treated as once functional but now vestigial) may simply be logically independent, i.e., unrelated. The term "functional relationship," then, should mean "functional or dysfunctional," obviously excluding the nonfunctional.

What is meant by "social system"? For a concept so much in use, it is too little analyzed by any but the Parsonians, but we can assume from what is written about it that it refers to a relatively self-contained system, in that some relations of its parts to each other and to the system itself are not dependent on anything outside the system. Thus, as an analogy, the autonomic nervous system is a part of the body and cannot exist without the body, but makes up a relatively self-contained system within the larger system of the organism of which it is a part. One may speak, then, of a kinship system, a caste system, or *the* social system, meaning *a* society.

A social system or society is characterized at least by (1) a dependence of the parts on each other (interdependence), (2) a relative independence for some purposes of anything outside the system, (3) shared symbols and values, which give meaning to situations, and (4) the shared ends and obligations I have discussed. In a kinship system, for example, the people, like all people, are dependent for their very lives on the growing or catching and distributing of food, the legal structure and its police auxiliary, exchange of commodities, and so on. But blood and marriage relationships are defined within the system, depend on each other, and are independent to that extent of anything outside it. And

*A. R. Radcliffe-Brown in *American Anthropologist,* Vol. 37 (1935), p. 396

shared symbols and values make the system intelligible and reinforce expected behavior.

Functional relationships are to be found within each of the
characteristics of a social system stated above. Obviously, in
(1), the dependence of parts on each other is a functional relationship. What other dependence of parts could there be in a social
system? In (3), symbols and values can be treated as functional,
dysfunctional, or nonfunctional for one another, yet these terms
are often only the social and psychological counterparts of logical
consistency, inconsistency, and independence. Persumably, if value
A is consistent with value B, they will function to support each
other in the mind of a man who holds both values. Irrationality is
everywhere, though, and the logical support A gives B may not be
paralleled by psychological support. Also, if A were inconsistent
with B, and were suddenly introduced into a formal system including B, it would be logically disastrous, but if A were accepted
by a mind already believing B, it might not—for a while, at least
—prove dysfunctional.

Relations between items in (1) and items in (3) may also be
functional relationships. Symbols and values may be functional or
dysfunctional for the dependence of the parts of a social system
on each other, and that dependence may be functional or dysfunctional for the use of the symbols and the belief in the values. A
high evaluation of centralized economic planning is dysfunctional
for a market economy, but the great success of the latter may
erode the evaluation. Items in (4), I have already argued in other
words, may be functional, dysfunctional, or nonfunctional for all
the others. When they work properly they, or substitutes that
work as well (functional alternatives), are indispensable functions.
When they are nonfunctional or dysfunctional, criticism may produce functional alternatives. I hope this is an adequate translation
into the language of functionalism.

By insisting on obligations and shared ends as parts of a
social system, we add categories otherwise neglected by functional
theory and are able to deal more precisely with a subject matter
that can, and should, be studied in sociology. I will return to the
subject matter of sociological study later in this chapter. For the
moment it is enough to point out that functionalists have used our

number (3), shared symbols and values, to explain kinds of functional and dysfunctional behavior, such as human dedication and opposition which have deep moral elements not fully translatable into symbols and values. Nor will conditioning and habituation serve as categories of explanation for such behavior. Talk about conditioning and habituation, without a moral dimension, can either lead to determinism, whose weaknesses have been explored in our first two chapters or, like determinism, reduce people to so many cogs in the social machine.

Number (2) is necessarily a little different from (1) and (3) in the matter of functional relationships, and is perhaps neglected by functionalists. Of course, items in (2) may be functional or dysfunctional for each other, but that is in a context, for the functionalist, not under consideration at the moment, since the set of related terms is outside the system with which we are concerned. If we consider such items at all it is because they are sometimes functional or dysfunctional for items in our system or for the system itself. Otherwise, they may be lumped with all other irrelevant matters as nonfunctional.

Two caveats may be in order here. First, the search for functional relationships, like the explanation of social change, may be hampered by a mistaken biological analogy: reasons for both the maintenance of the system and its changes may be sought too exclusively in the nature of the system itself. Popular historical explanation, in terms, for example, of the youth or age of a society, is often an error of the same sort. The health, or maintenance, of the physical organism seems explicable by noting the proper function of its parts. Why not the "health" (or continuance) of the social "organism"? What about social arteriosclerosis in an aging society? But even when we catalogue the functioning of the body's organs, as a physician might, we too readily overlook the environment. Respiration is splendid, digestion excellent; so the patient is healthy. But what does he breathe and what does he eat? Part of his respiratory and digestive health is due to the oxygen content of the air and the nutritive value of the food.[*] And the quality of the air can be, and in many places is, spoiled by chemicals. Obviously this is only a beginning; we may have to

[*]See C. H. Waddington: *The Ethical Animal,* New York: Atheneum, 1961.

go much farther in locating conditions of health and illness. And in society, by the same token, what is functional or dysfunctional for a given system is often no part of the system itself.

Second, seeking the causes of social change on the analogy of evolution may lead to the same sort of error (staying within the system), in this case because we look too hard for the equivalent of mutations based on the genetic lottery. Changes in society are much less likely to be inherent in the nature of the thing changing than in its social environment.* Kinship rules, for example, are less likely to change because of something in their own essence, or because of relations within the kinship system, than because of political revolution, the economic hardships of an impoverished aristocracy, or social mobility based on education and merit.

Now what kind of social phenomenon can be functional? Robert K. Merton emphasizes its standardized, or patterned and repetitive, character. Thus it is not a unique act by a person, but a social pattern, a role, a norm, an organization, a structure. And any of these may, in its effects on a system, be functional, dysfunctional, and nonfunctional at the same time. The question will then be which effect is which. A state religion, for example, may unify the nation by providing a stable set of norms, or values, which are widely accepted. In that respect it is functional. But it will be dysfunctional if membership in it is a condition of holding public office and many gifted people are not, and do not become, members. Finally, it *may* be nonfunctional in its particular doctrine of the Trinity.

There is a widely accepted distinction in contemporary sociology between what is intended by an action and everything else that happens as a result of it, a distinction between individual purpose and motive on the one hand and unintended social function on the other. Merton makes the distinction in terms of manifest and latent functions, manifest functions being "those objective consquences contributing to the adjustment or adaptation of the system which are intended and recognized by participants in the system," and latent functions being "those which are neither in-

*See Kenneth E. Bock: "Evolution, Function, and Change," *American Sociological Review,* April 1963.

tended nor recognized."* I shall use this distinction until, in the next chapter, it is reformulated.

The puzzles about functionalism that bother many social theorists and sociologists radiate, I think, from concern with the view of man and society that is presupposed by the basic functionalist argument rather than by what is stated. Since the vague thesis that society is the subject matter of sociology is generally assumed, functionalism has readily been understood as an empirical hypothesis about society. Taken as such, it has an extreme and moderate wing. The extremists find everything in society to be functional (some, occasionally, find things dysfunctional); the moderates see both function and dysfunction and, although they may not be very interested in the category, insist that there may be nonfunction. Malinowski was willing to state the extremist thesis openly; others presuppose it in particular studies. Evidence that the extreme position is presupposed is, probably, either "discovery" that the most unlikely behavior (almost anything one can imagine) is somehow functional for man or society, or a claim that A is functional when as good (or as poor) a case can be made for non-A.

As an example, a discussion of the relations of prejudice (against Jews, Negroes, and the foreign-born) to vertical mobility in the United States, concludes that those moving up or down the social ladder are more likely to be prejudiced than those who are relatively stationary. The authors discuss Park** and Williams† on the subject, and restate what they take to be their thesis: "... prejudice tends to be maintained or increased among groups in the process of securing or enhancing their social status or prestige." Then they expand the thesis: "This hypothesis applies to mobile groups in relatively marginal statuses irrespective of their present position or the direction of their mobility."

On the basis of this, the authors conclude:

> Thus prejudiced attitudes as yielded by our findings have a functional significance. They function, as attitudinal

*Social Theory and Social Structure, Glencoe, Ill.: Free Press, 1951, p. 35.

**Robert E. Park, Race and Culture, Glencoe: Free Press, 1950.

†Robin M. Williams, The Reduction of Intergroup Tensions: A Survey of Research, New York: Social Science Research Council, 1947.

props, to maintain at higher levels the subjectively felt diminishing prestige of groups objectively descending in the social status ladder, as well as to release tensions arising from the accompanying frustrating consequences of failing to succeed. In the case of groups objectively rising in social status, such attitudes function to enhance and secure their newly-won prestige which they subjectively feel to be raised but find threatened or unstable.*

The first thing that strikes the reader is that the conclusion is not justified by the evidence. Even if it is true that prejudice is maintained or increased among marginal groups going up or down the social ladder, it doesn't follow from that alone that it is functional (the word is apparently psychological here as well as sociological) for them. To begin with, there is an inherent difficulty of social science: one cannot find out how the people involved behave in the absence of the condition in question when it is nowhere absent. So we cannot learn whether, if such people had no prejudice,, they would feel more "threatened or unstable." But even within the limits of possible evidence, we would have to find out if members of mobile groups who are more prejudiced suffer fewer tensions when they go downward and feel less threatened when they go upward, than members of the same groups who are less prejudiced. But this sort of criticism is only incidental to my main concern.

Another criticism is more central, although still not my chief point. Suppose we were to discover that Americans traveling abroad for the first time regularly carried more baggage than they needed. We could call that functional, saying that it lessened the insecurity of being in a strange land by making people feel they were equipped, physically at least, for any possible circumstances. But instead, it might be dysfunctional, making them feel encumbered, insufficiently mobile, ill at ease. Why would anyone choose the first hypothesis? It has no more evidence in its favor than the second, for we have not talked to travelers about it. It is no more plausible on the face of a mere correlation. Probably—and this is

*Joseph Greenblum and Leonard I. Pearlin, "Vertical Mobility and Prejudice: A Socio-Psychological Analysis," in Reinhard Bendix and Seymour Martin Lipset, editors, *Class, Status, and Power,* Glencoe, Ill.: Free Press, 1953, pp. 486-487.

the point—the first hypothesis would be chosen by people who move intellectually from a presupposition that does make it seem plausible: that everything we do is somehow functional.

This extremist belief has a ring of truth just because everything is grist for the mill of some purpose and can be so interpreted by the exercise of ingenuity. Why do so many people play golf? Golf is relaxing and healthy. It is, of course, but only if we make it so. It may be distracting and enervating. It may be neither. The last resort of the extremist position is the belief that people don't do things that yield no satisfaction (that may be what Talcott Parsons means by saying that actors in a social system are motivated by a tendency to the "optimization of gratification") and, by analogy, things don't occur and persist in society if they have no function. Now the former is not true: people are habituated to endless rounds of activity that yield no satisfaction or less satisfaction than alternate possibilities. And the latter is probably not true. Almost anything can and does occur socially, and persistence may be due to habit, inertia, or accident. The one way to save this belief from refutation is to define its terms so negative evidence is inadmissible. For example, one can define "satisfaction" as that which is yielded by all action. But that is scarcely a miracle of scientific procedure.

Nonetheless, the extremist position dies hard, although there may be few today who would advocate it explicitly. Malinowski, who did, said that ". . . in every type of civilization, every custom, material object, idea and belief fulfills some vital function, has some task to accomplish, represents an indispensable part within a working whole."* With what limited set of categories did Malinowski come to so sweeping a conclusion? It is like a physicist saying that he tries to find connections among physical occurrences, and concluding that ours is, therefore, an ordered universe in which everything is connected to the whole. The conclusion in both cases is non sequitur. We find what can be found. We do not have to assume, because we find something has a function, that everything has.

Suppose we inquire into the function of the screaming, bell-ringing, snake-dancing behavior of the delegates at national party

---

*Encyclopaedia Britannica, 14th ed. Supplementary Volume I, 1936, s.v. "Anthropology."

conventions for nomination of a president and vice-president. Might we not say that it is a preliminary to the enthusiasm necessary in the coming campaign, that it is an expression of the importance to American politics of the common man, and so is a political ritual, or that it provides, under American conditions, the cohesiveness that knits political parties into some unity? Yet if political conventions were conducted with the greatest surface earnestness and decorum, would we not say with equal conviction that the function of such recurrent behavior was to underline the awful solemnity of the occasion, that it expresses the seriousness with which Americans cherish their right of political choice, or that it provides the iron and discipline that knits political parties?

It is entirely possible, although probably not true, that no one at such conventions enjoys the behavior into which he is forced. It is probable that most Americans regard the conduct of the delegates as becoming only to a circus (that is, if they think about it at all). And it is nearly certain that Europeans treat the whole thing as ludicrous and barbaric. There is nothing in the nature of the case that forbids it to be another instance, among perhaps countless instances, in which a pattern once established in some adventitious way is sanctified as a tradition and continues despite rational disapproval.

The two types of function, consequences of the existent raucous convention and consequences of the imagined decorous one, could both be useful for political parties and American society and yet be in conflict. That is, the functions of one style of convention are quite opposed to the functions of the other, yet both might have some value for the system, or could be interpreted as having value, i.e., being functional. What is critical about this is the ease with which ingenuity can convert any social phenomenon into theoretical gold. The fault is in Malinowski's postulate, which leaves no room for accident, inertia, habit, indolence, or folly in social survival. Again, this may be based on an evolutionary thesis, so ingrained in the mind that it is applied to society unreflectively: the survival of the fittest. Obviously, one might say, the fittest social items are the functional ones and when an item survives for many years, it is functional. But only on Malinowski's postulate, and without evidence.

Moderate functionalists think all social activity has

functional or dysfunctional consequences and add, with Merton: "There is also the empirical possibility of *nonfunctional* consequences, which are simply irrelevant to the system under consideration."* But are they nonfunctional from their inception? It is easy to beg the question, and so avoid empirical examination. Many theorists, confronted by a social pattern that cannot be explained as functional no matter how much ingenuity they expend, will insist that it must be vestigial, like the human appendix, thus assuming that the only nonfunctional activities which survive are those that once had positive functions. Does this presuppose, further, that social patterns come into existence because, and only because, of societal needs, and may later remain as vestigial, becoming nonfunctional or dysfunctional? Such a presupposition makes the functional (probably the latently functional, because of other beliefs) basic, and both logically and temporally prior to other patterns.

So it seems fair to say that functionalism as a theory of society is too easy to use as explanation and may lead to thoroughly unwarranted conclusions. Extreme functionalism is a kind of social metaphysics, something like the Great Chain of Being if that were applied only to society. The same sort of metaphysics applied to the universe would connect moral rules and celestial mechanics in a single whole whose parts are all dependent on each other.

One alternative to interpreting functionalism as a theory of society is to interpret it as a special method of investigation. On this score, several criticisms of functionalism** have been, I think, quite successful. I do not want to recapitulate what has been said in those criticisms, but I think we can conclude from them that functionalism as a method for the study of society is either no

*Merton, *op. cit.*, p. 51.

**The most revealing of these attacks from the standpoint of method are, perhaps, by Ernest Nagel in a symposium, "Problems of Concept and Theory Formation in the Social Sciences," in *Science, Language, and Human Rights* (Philadelphia, University of Pennsylvania Press, 1952), pp. 43-86, and by Carl G. Hempel, "The Logic of Functional Analysis," in Llewellyn Gross, ed., *Symposium on Sociological Theory* (Evanston, Row, Peterson and Co., 1959). A more elaborate statement by Ernest Nagel is in Chapter 10, "A Formalization of Function," of his book *Logic without Metaphysics* (Glencoe, Ill., Free Press, 1956).

different from scientific method itself or, if different, wrong. Some social scientists may decide, therefore, to give up functionalism altogether; others may relegate it to an important place in the development of sociology and anthropology, but find it without current value. A number of sociologists, despite the attacks, insist that they, and most of their colleagues as well, remain practicing functionalists. This is close to the truth, for we are entitled to argue only that functionalism is neither true as a general theory of society nor valid as a special method of social science. What should become clear is something else entirely: functionalism has to do with the definition of society, and so with the subject matter of sociology, as it has to do with the definition of politics, and so with the subject matter of political science.

　　Functionalism is to the study of social structures as physiology is to anatomy. Structural study—the anatomy of society—has a long history in sociology and anthropology, and is still rather dominant in political science. The functional concern is with the ways in which structures operate, especially in their consequences to themselves and the other structures, activities, and functions of society. This concern is not with isolated, unrelated human actions, nor with individual psychology, but rather with the effects of patterns of action on the maintenance, adjustment, disorganization, and destruction of such things as groups, social structures, roles, and norms. So it is not a theory of society nor a new method; it is a shift in attention, or a widening of attention, to new subject matter. Implicitly at least it is a new definition of a subject.

　　The subject matter of a science is not just a segment of the experiential flux, nor is it a number of discrete experiences. A subject matter is defined by the categories under which, or in accordance with which, we select the kinds of experience we intend to organize and explain. Such categories may be, as I have said, matter and motion, or compounds, elements, and chemical transformation. But whatever they are, they embrace what we want to know. And what we want to know may—and does— change in the course of history. Alchemy is presumed to have a place in the development of chemistry, but the very appearance of chemistry required a shift in attention, a choice of subject matter under the heading of new categories.

Functionalism, I am proposing, should be interpreted as just such a shift in attention, and functional theory, when it is at all useful, as a clarification of the categories which embrace a new subject matter. Much structural study has been and will continue to be valuable to it. The details of a political constitution, for example, may be closely related to the way the constitution functions. Or they may be nearly irrelevant, as Section Two of the Fourteenth Amendment to the Constitution of the United States has for so long been irrelevant.

There are always matters to which we have not attended scientifically. To discover how to do so is to discover a new science. But these matters can rarely any longer be physical objects, or governments, or international trade. Civilization is too old for many such new subjects. To discover a new field of study today is normally to discover new ways of studying the old subjects, or rather to study them under new categories, which point to neglected relationships. Sometimes this requires the use of several already established disciplines, as in physical chemistry and biophysics, or economic history and political sociology. Sometimes, as in sociology proper, there is first a feeling that something significant has been neglected, then an attempt to state it, which results in vague but exciting definition, and finally a gradual coming to focus. For Comte and Spenser, sociology was a kind of unified social science, and the desire for a single science of society has marked, more or less strongly, the work of Marx, Weber, and Parsons. Long before any of these, Plato and Aristotle had conceived a unitary social science, but it was politics, not sociology. The difference is the place assigned to reason and to rational control in society. Even when, in the Machiavellians if not Machiavelli, the study of politics became more limited in scope, it retained the sovereignty of reason, but redefined reason to exclude the consideration of ends (and so of ethics) which were simply assumed to be the attainment and maintenance of power, to them the prime category of politics.

Sociology attained a focus, which it still retains, as the study of group "life" and relations. This meant the study of institutions and processes under the head of new categories, and so it meant attention to neglected aspects and relationships. The categories included group interactions, system, rank, institutions, status, and role. Particular empirical studies were the hallmark of American sociology, as data-gathering and classification were once the hallmark of anthropology. But the concept of culture became sufficiently important so that more and more there was an attempt to relate processes to each other, to show how the group or society or culture was maintained and adjusted, or disorganized, by social activities within it. The materials gathered by particular studies can be used regularly in a functional analysis of society, and the needs of that analysis can give direction to new empirical research.

If I am right that the idea of functionalism is the idea of a subject, it is clear why the literature reveals so many sociologists and social anthropologists in fact concentrating —however unwittingly—on latent functions. Manifest functions are, for the most part, the concern of other disciplines. We intend specific effects by the laws we make, the things we produce, the offices we seek. Here we enter the realm of politics, and with it political science, for that is where the ways of attaining intended effects* are studied regularly. Such a study is one of means and ends. Sociology, however, should be concerned mostly with the context within which we choose means to yield our ends. This does not itself involve means and ends so much as causes and effects, latent functions rather than manifest functions. For the context of our actions is usually an inherited and continuing social structure that we did not ourselves make, whose existence is in those patterns of action that have not been deliberately contrived in our time to yield ends we desire. When we do alter any of these patterns deliberately, the altered pattern may itself acquire latent functions discoverable by sociological study. Democratic government in America, for example, was for the most part deliberately contrived, and many of its consequences were intended. But surely not all.

It may seem that the very distinction between society and politics made, for the moment, in terms of latent and manifest

---

*"The ability to attain intended effects" is also a common definition of power, from Hobbes to Russell, and power in society is usually thought of as a political category, although it is being studied increasingly by political sociologists.

functions, neglects the economy, religion, and perhaps other institutions and structured activities. After all, there are separate intellectual disciplines, such as economics, for the study of these
matters. But that is because all social institutions and structured
activities, studied in themselves, escape from the trammels of sociology and political science as they are normally defined. Only one
aspect of religion is studied by sociology, and the formal organization of churches is sufficiently a matter of government to be
studied by political science; much remains of religion as a subject
matter for study that cannot be treated by sociology or political
science. The same is true of the economy. The formal organization
of business corporations may be studied usefully by the methods
and categories of political science; informal organization and latent
functions may be studied by sociology; but technical economic
matters require another discipline.

Yet the parceling out of social activities to different intellectual subject matters does not mean the activities themselves are
not divisible into the social and the political. Managerial functions
are political, in my sense of the word; they are like the decisions
and carrying out of decisions that characterize so much of private
life, except that they are decisions for a group or organization;
that is what makes them political. Other functions of structured
activities are social, even though they require more than sociological categories and methods to study them. And some aspects of
institutions and structured activities are humanistic.

Society and politics are shot through with moral concerns.
Functionalism, as I have treated it here, embraces the subject
matter of both sociology and political science, since it includes the
latent functions that define society and the manifest functions
that define politics. From the standpoint of the moral, *conventional morality is social and critical morality is political,* at least in
the large sense of "political" which goes beyond nations, prov-
inces, and cities, and deals with the governance of all groups.

As I have argued, conventional morality has to be discovered; it is latent in the organization of groups. When conventional morality is discovered, it may merely be noted or mentioned, or it may be formally stated with some care. In the latter
case, even though there is no idea that the discovered morality be
deliberately changed, the statement itself probably brings some

change, at least in precision, from the latent obligation; and once conventional morality is conscious, it is rationally corrigible and is in process of becoming critical morality. Both critical morality and enunciated conventional morality are part of the politics of groups, for they are the basis of order and rule, and may become the basis of dissent; also they are in the realm of reason and attempted control.

More concretely, if A takes a job, and so is a member of a business organization, how much is he told of the obligations that go with his new membership and of the position he holds in the organization? He may be told he should file insurance claims, come to work at 9 A.M. and depart at 5 P.M., and who his ostensible superiors are. A usually discovers for himself what the chain of command is (really, not ostensibly), how best to file claims, what to tell clients, superiors, and inferiors, and on what occasions, in short, to whom he is obligated to do what as a result of his responsibility to the organization. He must also learn—this is somewhat separate—how to fill the role that goes with his status, *how* to talk to clients, superiors, and inferiors, how close his social relations to them should be, even perhaps what he should wear. Role is not obligation, but the manners thought appropriate to particular obligations.

Having discovered his latent obligations ("latent" is relative; what I don't know you may), A may adapt excellently to his job, or he may give it up because of what he has learned. He may even keep the job and try to alter his obligations which, he finds, do not yield ends he shares. This is a relatively trivial instance, perhaps clearer because of its triviality. But on a large scale, sociology could discover latent obligations in all manner of groups and in society itself. A new breed of social scientists may be required to do this, and by doing it allow moral philosophy and politics to criticize obligation. Yet by uncovering latent obligation and explaining it, sociologists would be doing what is in the nature of their discipline: discovering what exists in human life that is functional, dysfunctional, or nonfunctional for the groups in which we have our being.

CHAPTER NINE

Society, Politics, and Morality

I have been using "latent and manifest functions" to describe, temporarily, the realms of society and politics, but I am not happy with the idea of function as it is normally stated or with the distinction between manifest and latent functions as it is usually drawn. So I will make five more points in criticism, discuss function again, and make a new distinction.

(1) The definition of functions as "consequences which make for the adjustment or adaptation of a given system" removes attention from adjustment and adaptation of parts of a system to other parts. Of course, moderate functionalists are fully aware that a consequence may be functional for one group in a society and dysfunctional for another, but they tend to treat such groups as units, or small systems. What I am objecting to may be too rigid a classification, so that every logical class sounds like a social system. If a shift in academic values brings increased pay to junior teachers, it is all right to say that this consequence of the new values is functional for junior teachers, but the class of junior teachers is not thereby converted into a system. In study of society and politics we need concern with the consequences of human action for all social relations, processes, groups, and classes, whether or not they constitute systems of some sort.

(2) The interest of the traditional functionalist in the survival of social structures leads directly to his concern with adjustment and adaptation. His assumption seems to be that in a changing world those structures survive which can be adjusted to new circumstances and to which we can adapt our behavior. Offhand, it seems a reasonable enough assumption, but it leads to

difficulties, for the same thing may be directly functional yet indirectly dysfunctional for the same structure. This is readily seen when what is directly functional for A is dysfunctional for a larger structure, B, of which A is a part. The consequence of the dysfunction for B may be later, or indirect, dysfunction for A. So the belief in extreme predestination may have been functional at the time for the logic and persuasiveness of seventeenth-century Jansenism but it was dysfunctional for the Roman Catholic Church as a whole, of which Jansenism was a part. One result was that pope and king condemned Jansenism and virtually destroyed it.

(3) It may not be clear when a structure or system that undergoes adjustment is still the same structure or system that existed before the adjustment or when the alteration is so great that, in effect, the consequence is a different structure. This is especially serious when the word "functional" implies survival. "Survival" itself need never be used although it is at issue, for "adjustment and adaptation of *the system*" implies that it is the same system afterward that it was before. Of course, a social scientist who finds that something is functional for a given system may argue that it is an integral part of the system itself, contributing to a continuing adjustment which is in the nature of the system, such as the price mechanism in a competitive economy. My question has really to do with adjustments so good that they become improvements, and with adjustments (probably deliberate) introduced in critical circumstances. In the former case, increased economic productivity might be functional for a mercantile economy, but if the productivity increased extravagantly might it not help convert the mercantilist into a capitalist economy? In the latter case, if French citizens had become British subjects in World War II, as Winston Churchill proposed, that presumably would have been functional for both nations in their terrible struggle for survival. But would they have remained the same nations? I think it most unlikely.

(4) Perhaps most important for this argument, it does not seem to me often possible to distinguish manifest from latent functions at all. When we speak of manifest functions as having consequences "which are intended and recognized by participants in the system," we must ask *which* participants. If the answer is

all, there may be few manifest functions in a particular system because of widespread ignorance and stupidity among the participants. When we define latent functions as "neither intended nor recognized" by participants in the system, we must ask again *which* participants. Some people, after all, see more than others, so some participants may intend and recognize consequences that others never perceive. What proportion of perceptive participants will lead us to deny that a particular function is latent? It has been argued that college sororities in the United States were, manifestly, places of residence and companionship but, latently, controllers of courtship and marriage.* It turns out, of course, that many alumnae, who remain members of their sororities and usually dominate them, are quite aware of the sororities' "latent" function and act deliberately to retain and improve it. The same is probably true of some undergraduates.

Such a case strikes me not as a matter of latent function at all, but of Machiavellianism. The Machiavellian destroys the distinction between manifest and latent by his regular practice, which is to do things to attain ends he either never mentions or actually denies, while professing his sole concern with other ends, in which he wants everyone else to believe. What is latent function to most participants in a system may be quite manifest to the real or would-be manipulators of the system, who hide the former by emphasizing entirely different functions, which then occupy everyone's attention.

E. Digby Baltzell** makes much of the fact that metropolitan men's clubs provide the scene for important business and financial transactions. Cecil Rhodes got control of De Beers, and so of the world's diamond market, at the Kimberley Club; J. P. Morgan and Charles Schwab planned the steel trust during a private dinner at the University Club in New York. The clubs, however, like sororities, defend their existence almost solely in terms of their social functions and, because for purely social purposes one should be able to choose only the kinds of associates he likes, the clubs have a splendid excuse for barring Jews, Negroes, and even Catholics. Clearly one result, the exclusion of Jews from the highest level of

*John Finley Scott, "The American College Sorority," *American Sociological Review* (August, 1965).

**The *Protestant Establishment* (New York, Random House, 1964).

financial decision and a concomitant restriction of their numbers in top banking and business executive circles, may be thought of as a latent function of metropolitan men's clubs. But some club members not only recognize but intend these consequences by the membership rules on which they insist. It may even be the case that these "latent" functions are the primary (although probably not the only) intention of many who support the rules, who have discovered in them one way of eliminating competitors and of creating a kind of caste system at the upper levels of American business.

(5) Finally, there is an intriguing little paradox involved in the phrase "participants in the system." When the social scientist "recognizes" and describes a latent function, he may argue that it does not therefore cease to be latent, now that it is recognized, for he himself is not a participant in the system. But if he is studying, let us say, marriage and the family, and he is a married man with children, in what sense is he not a participant in the system? In the sense that *qua* social scientist he is an outside observer. Yet, when he comes home at night one cannot expect him, in his capacity as paterfamilias, to forget totally what he recognized in his office in his capacity as social scientist. And when he publishes his findings we do not forbid married men to read them. So there may be many "participants" in the system who "recognize" what they are not supposed to.

I think it fair to conclude that (1) the idea of the functional (and with it the idea of the dysfunctional) is flawed by the concept of "social systems" and the concept of "survival," to both of which it is related by definition, and (2) the distinction between manifest and latent may be impossible to make and, when it can be made, difficult to apply. Perhaps the very rigor of the definitions is at fault, social material being as fluid as it is. The idea of social function is, after all, that of a kind of behavior, the behavior of "social items" rather than of individual people. But it is not the idea of social behavior *per se*; it is social behavior considered in terms of somewhat regular or recurrent consequences, just as "conduct" is not human behavior *per se,* but human behavior considered in terms of moral qualities and obligations. Function is not just cause and effect, because it includes a number of purposive human acts that are recognizable as a pattern of social behavior, in addition to the regular consequences of those acts. Function is not just means and ends, in part because the consequences are not always deliberate goals. One may say that the (or a) function of marriage is to care for children, and in saying that one says something that is not quite cause and effect or means and ends but their parallel in social behavior.

As for the functional and the dysfunctional, it is probably sufficient to treat that as functional which maintains or promotes a particular end and that as dysfunctional which impedes or hampers it. So long as one specifies the end to which the terms apply, those terms can be used fruitfully. And there is great virtue in treating what is functional for the survival of a system quite separately from other sorts of functions. For example, technical innovations under government supervision to provide for smog control and so full use of gasoline by the automobile engine might be functional for the production of Ford cars (to say nothing of clean air), but the Ford Corporation and its automobile plants, as systems, would undergo a sea change.

Robert Merton's definition of functions as "consequences contributing to the adjustment of the system" could easily include obligations and shared ends. And those can be, as I pointed out, functional, dysfunctional, or nonfunctional. But to keep "function" as contribution to the maintenance of "the system" is to limit the use and value of "function" as a social category. For it chooses one end, granted a major one, as *the* end for the study of which sociology exists. And if the categories of morality were to be added to other social categories to increase the scope and decrease the triviality of sociological study, the single end would limit the social study of morality, leaving it much less than I have suggested it should be.

The unworkable distinction between manifest and latent functions needs replacement by another distinction because there is indeed a difference in types of function which "manifest" and "latent" were supposed to mark. I should like to speak of overt, or primary, functions and covert, or secondary, functions. The criteria for distinguishing them can be stated rather generally: overt, or primary, functions are (1) intended; (2) avowed or publicly acknowledged; (3) higher in the order of value or obligation (on the part of most of those involved, members or participants) than other consequences; covert, or secondary, functions are those which do not meet all three criteria for overt functions, especially the second. Some elaboration may be useful.

Clearly, not all group members or participants in a structured activity have the same order of valued or obligatory consequences. A particular graduate student in an American university may, at a given time, order the desired consequences of his study in the following way: (1) to avoid conscription; (2) to continue to be supported by his parents for some time. And there may be no other consequences he desires, not even a graduate degree. So the criterion of avowal must be taken to mean the ordinarily acknowledged function or functions of any social structure or activity, no matter what particular people see or seek in it for themselves. In the sense I intend this, the overt function of schools is to educate, that is, the ways in which schools function should yield education as an end. And even if the majority of students in our colleges were concerned with attaining a degree only as a condition of higher income, the function highest in the order of obligation or value of those who maintain schools (citizens, taxpayers, teachers, etc.) is that colleges and universities provide education. That is what they intend them to do, and is one reason they maintain them. Even the student whose primary desire is something other than education usually knows what the acknowledged function of the schools is, probably agrees it is their primary obligation, and realizes that he is perverting it. That is, such a student is in a way Machiavellian and, like all Machiavellians, probably maintains openly that he seeks A, while in secret he desires B.

Machiavellianism is perhaps rare enough in its pure form but, diluted, it is everywhere. It is the model of much personal use of the institutions and structures of society. Machiavellianism is the opposite of enlightened self-interest: the Machiavellian does not desire ˊfor others the good he seeks for himself, not even as a condition of his own good. But he is not indifferent to the desires of others; he needs them to want what he does not. Unless they seek and intend something else, public and avowed, or unless, perhaps with some ambivalence, they say they seek it, as he does, his chances of attaining his own ends are slight. The pure Machiavellian prospers only when there are few pure Machiavellians, for his great **advantage** over others is that they are more honest than he. Otherwise he would have to match wits with them and that might give him no advantage at all. The ordinary, or diluted, Machiavellian prospers only when others proclaim, with him, a desire for A, even though it may be B they want (whether they are conscious of it or not), for that allows the continuance of an institution or structure he can use to his own ends. Even if a large number of people are somewhat hypocritical about their avowal of A, and A is part of public morality, the institution that is supposed to yield A has every possibility of survival. A case in point is the institution of marriage in times when it is commonly dishonored in the breach but avowed in the observance.

So both A and B are in different ways desired by Machiavellians because, even though they want B for themselves they want A, too: they need its existence and they need others to desire A, even if there is some pretense in almost everybody's avowal of it. If others did not desire A, or if A could not be attained, the Machiavellian's chance of attaining B would be diminished: e.g., if it became clear that graduate schools could not or did not educate their students, but were primarily devices for avoiding military service, they would in all probability be drastically changed. Further, A, the avowed consequence, is approximately the same for everybody, but B varies from person to person. Put differently, there is a uniform A (or A's) but usually such a variety of B's that they may be thought of better as B_1, B_2, B_3 ... So that three people desiring respectively B_1, B_2, and B_3 would still avow A.

Any social institution or structure may at the same time yield A, overtly, and any or all B's, covertly. Covert functions range in their consequences from these intended but not publicly acknowledged B's to genuinely unintended and unrecognized consequences. An important kind of covert function, sometimes intended and recognized, is the result of informal organization. We can regard the formal organization of any social structure as an order of statuses and obligations designed to yield the structure's overt functions. The hierarchy and job assignments in a factory, the descending order from chief of staff to private soldier in an army, are formal organizations in the interest of overt functions. But personal relationships among factory employees and the accidental social structure of an officers' club are informal. They are adventitious to the formal design but not necessarily irrelevant to its purposes.

On occasion, informal organization brings change to overt function. The personal relations of factory employees may lead to a discussion of grievances and then to a production slowdown; an officers' club may breed a cabal; a faculty lounge may launch an educational reform. More commonly, informal organization yields covert functions which may be unintended or may be intended but not publicly avowed. As a particular officers' club in peacetime might lead to so desirable a social life that officers seek transfer to the military base in which it is housed, so a widespread, attractive social life for the officer corps in an army might bring recruitment of officer candidates who essentially desire that kind of life, however much they insist publicly that their recruitment is based on dedication to the defense of their country. And especially in the earlier part of the twentieth century, a worker might join a trade union primarily for greater power vis-à-vis his employers and, because of the union's study groups and fraternal circles, gain an education that changed his living habits and his ideas, including his beliefs about unionism.

The conclusion to be drawn from the argument so far should itself be a beginning for a new social and political analysis, since it points to the contexts and some of the terms to be used in that analysis. *Society is composed essentially of covert functions, dysfunctions, and nonfunctions, and politics is composed of overt functions, dysfunctions, and nonfunctions.* It seems to me that the subject matter of sociology proper emphasizes society thus defined and that the subject matter of political science proper emphasizes politics in this sense. Of course, political behavior may not, in any particular case, bring about the avowedly intended and fundamentally desired consequences that it seeks, and may even breed the nonfunctional, but such consequences are indeed intended. The Paris conferences of the United States and North Vietnam were, most of the time, nonfunctional, although intended as functional. The actual consequences, when not the intended ones, or the lack of consequences, must be studied in relation to the means employed, so that different means may be used if necessary. (Sometimes the nonfunctional is dysfunctional as well; the Paris talks may have prevented other and better action.) For politics is an area of purpose and control, of the deliberate manipulation of society to desired ends by way of obligation. When political science does attend to covert functions (it is already aware of their existence but not sure of their nature, so they are semi-overt), it does so to bring them into the context of politics, i.e., the context of rational control and overt obligation. And when sociology discovers and states covert functions, it prepares the way for politics and the conversion of covert into overt functions. This does not narrow sociology's subject matter, although it does change its momentary problems, because new overt functions create new covert functions.

To clarify this relation between overt and covert functions, it may be worth returning for a moment to Merton's language of manifest and latent functions. When that language is used, all functions are presumably either manifest or latent, yet in fact we encounter functions that have ceased to be latent but have not become manifest. In Merton's definitions, manifest functions "are intended and recognized by participants in the system," and latent functions "are neither intended nor recognized." Yet when sociologists discover latent functions and announce their findings, those functions are then recognized even by "participants in the system" but may still not be intended. Clearly, latent dysfunctions, when recognized, are usually not intended.

This new class of "social items," functions and dysfunctions recognized but not intended fits into the language of overt and covert functions as here described. Since covert functions range from those intended and recognized by some or all members, although not publicly acknowledged and avowed as the group's function, to those that are unintended and unrecognized, this new class may be characterized as recognized covert functions. Recognition of a covert function and the consequent articulation of it makes it an object of thought, renders it corrigible, and prepares it to become overt, to enter other overt functions, or to be rejected because it is not a means to shared ends or itself a shared end. Examples may be required to clarify this process.

A covert function of the first landing of men on the moon may have been a distraction of American attention from domestic problems. The summer of the first moonshot spawned less rioting, looting, and demonstrations than the summer before and the summer before that. Genuine social study of the shift in interest and the growth in national pride, to mention only two consequences of the moonshot, might have made clear the extent to which Americans were indeed distracted, as well as the kind of event that, in these circumstances, breeds distraction: its accomplishment, perhaps, its novelty, and its centrality in the attention of news media. There is also the question of its dysfunction, which could be studied equally well: how much embitterment resulted from the astronomical sums that were needed for the astronomical venture, sums which perhaps could have been spent on domestic problems and obligations.

We do not know what such studies might have revealed; they were not made. But had they been made and shown, say, that novelty and discovery, in the sense of landing for the first time on an untrodden shore, did indeed distract American attention from duties and other issues, and that embitterment that the resources (brains, time, energy, commitment, money) were not spent differently was felt by relatively few at first, but by many more as the glory dimmed, then there might be two important consequences. First, as the covert functions of the moonshot were discovered, or "recognized," the moral and political problems of moonshots would be clarified. The ends shared by the majority of Americans would be better understood, as well as the priorities they assigned to those ends. People who wanted those ends supported could plead for them; people who thought the ends shoddy or in conflict with obligation could oppose them. Government could fit its action to what it had learned, or make a strenuous effort to change the ends of its people. Possibly, government could make overt by its actions and statements that its concern was henceforth for space exploration and that the problems of earth would become the obligations of business.

Second, covert functions would then emerge from what was now overt. Those who had thought of the first moonshot as discovery, the beginning of the next stage for human life, and as almost necessary for the progress of science (the overt functions of that first moonshot) might have been sufficiently shaken by the revelation of the moonshot's covert functions to reconsider the moonshots to come. Those embittered by the resources used for space might be more embittered. Others would cling to the original intent and the overt functions of the moonshot and insist that we had barely started the new world and must continue, whatever individual tragedies might result. Covertly, the issue between those who wanted a new world in order to escape this one (that new world being to them the last great hope of earth, as once America had been), and those who wanted to make a stand here, and rid earth of its pestilences, would be joined. A covert function, or dysfunction, of the new governmental acts, would be an intellectual civil war, exhibiting great disaffection from the government. Ultimately, the government might fall or violence erupt.

Immediately the issues were implicitly joined, however unconsciously and covertly—the covert is society's unconscious—a matter of great importance was in the wings, to enter the stage of public action only when itself overt. For then the people inflamed by visions of the new frontier, the moon, had tacitly given up the earth as irredeemable and wanted our resources lavished on what might save mankind, while those who took their stand here, and thought the solution of human problems could only be postponed by new lands and a new frontier, insisted that we expend our resources here and now, and postpone the frontier.

Such an issue, joined covertly, would be a matter of values and ends, *leading to new obligations,* when that issue became overt. In the language of functionalism, there would be new functions and dysfunctions depending on who won out. In the moral language I have used, whoever won out, there would be a new conventional morality and another chance at creating critical morality.

If the example just suggested seems too fanciful, or if an implicit struggle in and for the minds of men does not seem a genuine covert function—it does to me—let me suggest a more obvious example. It will show how speculative is talk of the covert functions of organizations that do not yet exist. A well-recognized covert function of college education is that it keeps many thousands of young adults off the labor market. Since at graduation from secondary school, young men and women are without highly developed skills, they would have to compete for relatively unskilled jobs if they did not go on to college. Such jobs in a society as technical as ours are getting scarcer, so if no one, or very few, went on for further schooling after secondary school was finished, the economy might suffer seriously. At the least, wages would go down and there would be a high rate of unemployment.

If difficulties about studies, curricula, student rights and power, and other such matters brought the closing of many colleges, the government might have to reopen them or create new "colleges" which no longer had as their overt function the education of students or their preparation for graduate and professional schools. Instead, the "colleges" would have as their overt function keeping the young from the labor market, and all students might be subsidized. What went on in those "colleges" would not be study of the liberal arts or pre-professional training, but whatever captured the interest of "students." The covert functions of the new "colleges" are nearly unimaginable, but would probably include a trained distaste for systematic work in many "students." Relatively unskilled students would enter the labor market anyway, four years later, and for those trained to hate work, special positions with more fun than work or duty might have to be created. All this could suit the future economy better than flooding the labor market with untrained seventeen-year-olds. An alternative possibility, and a more likely one, I suspect, might be to forget education altogether, except for those needed in highly skilled professions, and convert most secondary school education into the training of skilled workers and of assistants to those in the professions.

However, much like *1984* my examples seem, the basic pattern, of which they are examples, emerges clearly enough. As secondary, or covert, functions of any kind are recognized by sociologists, the political scientists and politicians who attend to them may raise the question whether they should be controlled, altered, or eliminated by deliberate governmental action. If so, they enter political science and, if action is taken, they become part of the political process. Then, as a result of political action, still more secondary functions are created, adding to the context of the social and so to the subject matter of sociology, ideally conceived. Such constant interchange of subject and such change in the purpose and method of its study could be basic to the relationship between political science and sociology. If it were, we might develop new ideas about the relations between society and politics, national and international.

Society, as conceived by many sociologists, and the state as conceived by Plato (if we may for the moment think of the *polis*

as the state) are both all-inclusive contexts in relation to which all
human behavior has its meaning. But society dwarfs and fashions
man; the state is his instrument and serves his purposes. Society is
not a deliberate creation, but the state may be. Each (society and
state) is a context which is ultimate, but they are antithetical in
the meanings placed on their contents. From the standpoint of
society, the state is one of its important institutions. From the
standpoint of the state, society is the way men live together under
its guidance and in accordance with its laws. Society is not rational; the state is.

So long as there was a single social study, like Plato's or
Aristotle's, and perhaps Herbert Spencer's, the characteristics and
categories of society, politics, and morality were all used together
to deal with the social entity. For Plato and Aristotle and many
others, the "state" had an ethical purpose, and that justified its
existence. But when specialization entered the study of men living
together, categories and characteristics were sorted out: sociology
had one set, political science another, and ethics ceased to be a
social study. Each, then, has become a partial explanation of the
life of men together, an explanation of community from a single
standpoint. The standpoint of society too easily neglects purpose,
decision, will, and reason. The standpoint of the state too easily
neglects history, tradition, continuity, and irrationality. Social science must include both sets of categories as well as moral categories, which it usually avoids, if it is to explain the life of men
together.

The state is not the only context of politics, as I have argued, and political science is still too much restricted to the study
of official governments, national, local, and intermediate. But even
in that context, definitions of political science have tended to be
reductionist. For some, political science is a study of administration. But what is administered, by whom and for whom? Nor is
it sufficient to define political science simply as the study of government, for that neglects such concepts as nation, state, and sovereignty. To broaden the definition by making political science the
study of ruling or governing is still reductionist if what is meant
by those terms is power, and especially if power is thought to be
derived from force rather than from obligation.

Power has been a popular subject for many years, and traditional analyses of power are at hand to bolster the argument that power is the essence of politics and the real subject of political science. It seems suitably hard-headed to make that argument, and it sweeps away consideration of the moral and the purposive which have, to the hard-headed, no place in any science. Power is the ability to attain intended effects, or the control over means. Political science is concerned with power insofar as the means controlled are people or affect people. People may be employed as means through persuasion, obligation, or force, and many power-theorists regard force as the underlying political reality, the foundation of political power.

It is persuasive to argue that force is the basic political reality, for when all other attempts to mediate conflict fail, force seems the final resort. And the controller of the bayonet seems to be the holder of power. But the argument fails just there. If power comes from the point of the bayonet, why don't the wielders of the bayonet have final power? Because they obey orders. But what enforces those orders? Still greater power? Whose? We can scarcely argue that a ruler derives his power from the force he controls and that he controls it because of his power. The wielders of the bayonet must consent to obey, and they consent because of tradition or convention, fear, obligation, love, or loyalty. Power presupposes consent, or at least acquiescence, but consent does not presuppose power. It is true, as Max Weber says, that government has a monopoly of legitimate force at its command, but that is not, ultimately, why it is the government.

It is not even true that the political is just the mediation of conflicting interests, although that is closer to the mark. Of course, conflicting interests must be mediated if there is to be order and stability, and if there is no other successful mediation, the task falls on government. But even in the absence of conflict there are social problems to be solved and it is government's responsibility to see that they are solved.

Where does this leave us? It leaves us with a definition of the political as *the machinery of deliberate social decision,* and, in consequence, the administration of such decision, which, of course, requires power but also requires obligation. This may in-

volve, as I have said, decision *by* a whole society or group, but it
need not. Whoever makes the decisions, those decisions are *for* a
society or group. Thus politics is the instrument through which a
nation controls its destiny, so far as it may, or through which its
destiny is controlled, so far as it can be. Even those areas which
are left alone by government are left alone as the results of a
political decision, explicit or implicit, conscious or not. It is a
political decision, for example, that "Congress shall make no law
respecting an establishment of religion, or prohibiting the free exercise thereof." That is explicit, of course, in the American constitution. But is is an implicit political decision that our government
shall not choose partners in marriage. Plato would have thought
that decision scandalous: it substitutes inclination and passion for
a rational application of genetic knowledge. But the implicit decision to leave room for inclination is, in the end, also potentially
rational and deliberate, because it can be made explicit and then
revoked or affirmed.

   Robert A. Nisbet has been concerned to show that sociology
has inherited much of the outlook of political conservatism and
that its very categories (such as status, cohesion, adjustment, function, norm, ritual, symbol) were those of conservative politics in
the nineteenth century.* It is an important point to make. Conservatism posed an organic society, which was the result of ages of
adjustment and adaptation, against the liberal insistence on individual freedom and the value of the act of thought. Fichte, Hegel, De
Maistre, and Bosanquet developed the conservative thesis. Conservatism described man as social, made what he is, indeed made human, by the society in which he lives, and it characterized the
liberal description of man as based on a state of nature from
which man came forth into society fully developed, rational, with
values and interests already decided. Social man versus natural
man! The choice for some seemed easy to make. Sociologists and
anthropologists made it, and have been teaching generations of
students how man is socialized, how he adopts the norms of society, how he suffers anomically if he does not hold them firmly,
and how absurd is the notion of natural man. I will come to some
analysis of that notion indirectly.

   *"Conservatism and Sociology," *American Journal of Sociology* (September, 1952).

The issue between Conservatism and Liberalism (and between sociology and politics) is reason, and its place in society, for it is in part an argument about whether men can, collectively, guide their destinies. How well can men guide society if every act of thought reflects society? Under those circumstances, assumed by conservatives and many sociologists, no one man has much social effect. We have already seen the error in that belief. Here I want to show that, despite the many criticisms, it is still possible to talk about natural man and the value to society of the individual act of thought; but not literally in the old terms of the state of nature and the social contract.

The idea of zeitgeist, the spirit of the time determining all institutions and social behavior, has permeated the social sciences, the study of history, revolutionary movements, the sociology of knowledge, and much else. It appears in the concept of culture and in defenses of relativism, in Malinowski's functionalism, in the idea of socialization, in Marxism, and in discussions of social evolution. It is one reason that the importance of the individual to history and social action is so often minimized. But the boundaries of culture and zeitgeist must be drawn if human reason is not to be submerged.

We have learned from social science that science itself comes into existence under favorable social conditions, waxes and wanes as those conditions change, and presumably will disappear if the conditions change too much. We have learned, too, that the questions asked in science are often those posed by the social needs and pressures of the time. What must be kept clear is what science is, relative to the cultures in which it is generated. Newton, it has been claimed, worked only on problems important to the bourgeoisie in his time. But science is a transcultural intellectual process, a way of attaining statements that do not depend on culture or zeitgeist for their truth, even though they depend on them for their existence. That is, particular scientific investigations and statements might not be made without the presence of certain cultural conditions, but their truth or falsehood is independent of those conditions. Indeed, science requires of the scientist in his work the suppression of cultural and personal traits, and the use of what is common to all men, reason and observation. And the uses of reason and observation by any scientist are open to review by any qualified person, whatever his culture.

To repeat, science is a paradigm of reason, and science is
both culture-bound and time-bound so far as its existence is concerned and the choice of many of its problems, but it is neither in
the efficiency of its basic methods and the truth of its conclusions. Those are universal, they work or do not work, and are true
or false, anywhere at any time. In the distinction we usually make
between society and nature, science is (in its methods and conclusions) "natural." So is reason in all its other honest manifestations.
Logic is older than Socrates, and a valid conclusion was then and
is now valid, among American sociologists or Navajo witches. Indeed, many of the puzzles of the sociology of knowledge disappear when we understand that the social scientist is not, qua scientist, subject to the same social conditioning as the people he
studies. He is somewhat outside the society when he acts as scientist. Granted that science only appears under certain social conditions, once it does appear, the scientist is redeemed from cultural
pressures by the "natural," trans-cultural method he uses.

So the liberal, taking his stand on the "natural" act of
thought, is not annihilated by conservative or sociological argument. Just as the sociologist has accepted some conservative theses
and categories, for they help with his scientific business, so the
political scientist has accepted some liberal theses and categories,
for they help with his. The liberal emphasis on the individual act
of thought and on the guidance of life and society by rational
decision suits a study whose subject is decision and the carrying-
out of decision. The liberal provides a complement to the conservative, adding the natural light of reason to the weight of tradition
and culture; and political science can provide the same complement to sociology. But how can rational decision be made without
moral ends to aim at? And how can conventional morality be
accepted as aims without reason, which yields critical morality?

Unfortunately, today, many practical problems that call for
both sociological and political knowledge are treated with the
knowledge of only one, and with little knowledge of morality at
all, which should be basic to both studies. Segregation (and desegregation) in the United States has been treated by too many
people as a sociological issue alone, political decision has been
arrived at with too little political evidence and argument, and moral categories have been kept quite separate, although the issue is

fundamentally and overwhelmingly moral. International peace and world government have been too long the province of international lawyers and political scientists, and have become hopelessly bogged down in questions of power, sovereignty, and national interest, which are too narrowly political to be of much practical help.

Much has been made in our time of the need for community, for shared values, for stable relationships. From the standpoint of sociology, they are functional and they minimize anomy with its resultant disorganization and social malaise. It is often asked: what above all brings about normlessness? And it is sometimes answered: reliance on individual reason with its criticism of values, of religion, of rite and symbol, and its consequent erosion of the significance of life. This is not only said by social scientists, but by poets like Yeats and Eliot. Yet something of great importance is overlooked when this charge is made. Adequate socialization to a highly organized community may bring its members security, solidarity, a sense of the significance of life, and an ability to share the world of the community, but how well does it equip them to criticize their own community and its morals, to share the world of other communities, and to develop a critical morality and an international community? Perhaps men must be more highly individuated before they are prepared for international understanding. Surely they must be more highly individuated and critically obligated before they can be more rational. And this leads to a paradoxical truth: reason, above all, requires individuation, but brings men together as men, because they can agree on its conclusions, not just as members of the same society. Reason is even a necessary condition for disagreement to be clear, and so perhaps fruitful.

The use of reason in guiding collective destinies is politics, and political man is not pre-social natural man (a figment of the imagination or a logical postulate) but is ideally post-social natural man, man who has developed his rational faculties and can arrive at conclusions and even responsibilities that are trans-cultural, and so "natural." Perhaps George Santayana thought of politics in this large sense when he wrote, in a letter of December 6, 1905, to William James: "I am a Latin, and nothing seems serious to me except politics, except the sort of men your ideas will involve and the sort of happiness they will be capable of. The rest is exquisite moonshine."*

*Ralph Barton Perry, *The Thought and Character of William James.* Little, Brown, 1935, Vol. 2, p. 402.

CHAPTER TEN

Obligation in Our Time

Obligations may be covert, yet we have them. I have spoken of discovering existent obligation, because it is there to be found and is not like critical obligation, which we make. Existent obligation is sometimes hidden in the interstices of groups, remaining unarticulated but obeyed. When that is so, existent obligation may be discovered as covert functions are discovered, by comparing what the group does with its avowed and overt functions.

If a men's club where business is transacted had a perfect or near-perfect voting record in which all Jews proposed for membership have been rejected, then one can guess there is a covert obligation of club members to keep Jews out of the club, and that members feel the obligation whether or not they know they have it. On the basis of that guess, or hypothesis, one can make further studies to show that the obligation is felt.

This is opposed to the usual way of seeing obligation, in which the question is how accepted obligation becomes felt obligation. Here the question is how felt obligation is discovered intellectually, and is then accepted, discarded, or modified. But how can there be felt obligations without people knowing what they are? The answer is: in the same way that people recognize dogs without knowing what they are, that is, being able to define them. One "knows" many things by identifying and recognizing them, without being able to make statements about them. There are "proper" ways to behave, and people are expected to behave in those ways, although no one has said precisely what they are. In an expensive preparatory school, for example, there may be ways in which the scions of aristocratic families maintain a social distance from scholarship students of middle and lower-class families,

and teach them not to expect the company or friendship of aristocrats; yet to formulate and approve such conduct overtly might
give scandal. The students who behave "properly" have picked up
cues, imitated those they admire, and reinforced each other, without making their obligations overt.

The Decalogue exhorts people to honor their fathers and
mothers, but does not say in what that honor consists. Each culture, the anthropologist tells us, determines honor's content in its
own way. But is it ever fully specified? And does not each family
in our culture differ in some of the obligations that fall on the
children, having not only some expectations all its own, but
weighting similar obligations differently? Most obligations are intuited and felt, and are accepted only in the sense that we are
impelled to carry them out, not in the sense that we consciously
understand them. Yet if we could articulate them correctly, it is
quite conceivable that we would reject them, and be shamed. The
first step toward converting much existent morality into law or
into critical morality is making covert obligation overt.

Covert social functions, of course, have covert obligations,
but either covert functions are not their only source, or we must
expand the idea of covert functions to include the unarticulated
ways in which each group, and each group unit of an institution
(this business, this college, this family), behaves in regularly attaining ends which are themselves unformulated. Relations between faculty and administration, for example, vary greatly from
large schools to small ones and from those of great reputation to
those of none. But in addition each school may attain its ends or
remain what it is by certain functions of its own. These bring with
them obligations to behave toward administration or faculty in
ways not understood or felt by outsiders or new personnel, and
intuited vaguely after a time. Independence of mind may be
prized, for example, but only up to a point, and a school may
thrive on constant faculty challenge of administrative decision, until the issue is really serious. A member of the college's faculty
may feel the obligation to engage in these antics, without knowing
why, and find himself approved or threatened—in acceptance, promotion, salary—because of the skill with which he stands up to the
administration and then withdraws.

There are countless examples of the same kind, and they are

all part of morality. In the college just described, an honest man who senses what is expected of him will either resign or try to change the situation. There are other ways of supporting morale, and he should seek them. They bring other obligations, and he should urge them. But first and most important, probably in this and all similar cases, is the discovery and statement of what one is expected to do, and to what ends. That can bring intelligent and overt change, as opposed to covert change that might be as foolish as what already exists. When obligations are discovered and articulated, they leave the social and enter the political activity of the group; there the obligations are discussed and criticized, and changes in obligation are proposed. Acceptance or rejection of the changes are political in that decision is arrived at for the whole group through its process for making group decision. And fundamental to decision is knowledge of the limits of consensus at the time, plus the gravity of the situation, which may alter those limits.

If a faculty member, for example, in the college discussed above, finally gets clear the obligations that have made him unhappy, his first task is to state them and give evidence from college history that his statement is correct. Then he engages in essentially political activity: persuading others that he has perceived obligations correctly, convincing them that such obligations are ignoble and destructive of the proper ends of a college, and seeking, with his adherents, the machinery for change. There may be a college senate, or one may be created, there may be faculty powers for reorganization, or they may be demanded, and members of the administration and student body may be consulted. Finally, plans for restructuring power and decision-making can be proposed to existent or newly created decision-making bodies. The plans should be such that, if approved, the unpleasant obligations will be replaced by more suitable ones. In addition, the dissident faculty members will have to deal with the limits within which consensus can be reached at the moment. If the limits preclude acceptance of the new plan, threats of resignation may widen them. Should they not be widened even then, the enterprise has failed and those who made the threats are obligated to resign. Such threats are equivalent to promises and carry with them a personal obligation.

One problem of felt obligation that is seldom considered when motivation to carry out obligation is discussed, is the development of empathy. Empathy is usually treated in the context of aesthetics, where it also belongs. In aesthetics, it has to do with putting oneself into a work of art one has not made, or identifying with the protagonist or another character in a drama or novel. In daily life, empathy consists in identifying with another person or feeling what it would be like to be oneself in his circumstances. In morality, empathy or its absence affects conduct toward others.

We have obligations to behave in certain ways to others no matter how we feel about them, but the likelihood of behaving toward them as we ought often hinges on our feelings about them. If one is puritanical enough, or Christian enough, he might behave fully as well toward a known enemy as toward a friend. And a man with a strong sense of justice might even behave better toward people he dislikes, because he is on guard against the obvious possibility of treating them badly. In the ordinary case, though, being well disposed toward the object of our action makes it much easier to behave as we should.

The Golden Rule raises the question of empathy in a fundamental way. "Do unto others as you would have them do unto you" is easier to carry out if we know the others will have the opportunity to help or harm us, and we intend our behavior to placate possible enmity on their part, or to call to their attention an action of ours which demands gratitude, or implies that we may be in a position again to hurt or help them, and so constitutes a threat. But if we feel in these ways while acting according to the Golden Rule, we have perverted its assumption, that we are all brothers, and corrupted its meaning so it becomes, at best, a statement of enlightened self-interest and, at worst, advice on self-seeking.

But how can we carry out the Golden Rule unless we feel the brotherhood of man or empathize with others? If they are like us, or we identify with them or their circumstances, we can feel their pains and miseries, and even feel how they will respond to our behavior, because it is like the way we would respond, or as we can imagine their responses. And now the difficulty arises that we cannot empathize, without a real act of imagination, with what is unlike ourselves. There are ranges of empathy. Can we empathize with a dog? A horse? An angleworm? A gnat? A blade of grass? Children and poets may, occasionally, but what of the rest of us?

Can a man even empathize with all other men, of any condition, creed, and color? Could a feudal lord empathize with a serf or a master with a slave, as they could with those of equal rank, similar background, and identical conditions of life? What does the Marxist dichotomy of bourgeois and proletarian do to empathy in those who accept the dichotomy? Does the full possibility of feeling critical obligation depend on creating forms of equality among men? And is it possible that the basic form of equality is the human one of moral agency, with its attendant freedom and problems and agonies?

I suspect that empathy requires—except in unusual cases—the creation of some equalities in the human condition. Those already exist, of course, and in great but not sufficient measure: apart from biological likeness, we share membership in groups of all kinds with others, and within those groups we share statuses that are similarly ranked. These are the places where empathy is most marked, and these are the people with whom we most readily empathize, because they are most like ourselves. The Golden Rule, however, deals with all men, as does Kant's Categorical Imperative, and like the Categorical Imperative it is over-general. But it is, by implication, a statement that men are equal, or should be treated equally. Since they are not, in fact, equal, socially or biologically, we can maintain only that they are equal in the rights they ought to have—or do have, naturally—and appeal to a common humanity. Yet since that common humanity is an ideal, rather than a fact, it has to be created if it is to exist. At its basis is a common moral agency which also does not exist equally among men, but which we can bring into existence.

As far as felt obligation goes, much of it comes from empathy, and empathy was intensified and extended, I think, in the modern western world (I leave aside the question of other civilizations), through the reintroduction of the drama in the late Middle Ages, and the growth of other art forms. In our day, the cinema and the television play are only the drama in other media, as are the spectator sports, and the drama is central to the development of empathy because of the psychological process by which we identify with characters in it and live their lives in our imaginations. It is a training, I believe, which prepares people to empathize in real situations. The expert playgoer, the critic, and the philosopher of art may learn to check empathy, so that their judgment may be cooler and more fastidious, but typical members of the audience either empathize or lose in enjoyment.

When there was far less public entertainment, in the sixteenth and seventeenth centuries, the common people were, as Huizinga tells us in his *Waning of the Middle Ages,* restricted for their entertainment to church services, processions, and public displays by the executioner. Torture and death were a part of the regular fare of daily life and the executioner's skill in prolonging torture before killing was much admired. Was there empathy with the executioner? Probably. If so, his public may have enjoyed dreams in which they themselves inflicted the pain, as empathy today with the ball-player or the matador brings fantasies of performing his deeds. Sports range from the bloody, like bullfighting and boxing, to the genteel, like tennis, and empathy with their participants brings fantasies of all sorts. It is a moot question whether scenes of violence in sports or the drama makes spectators violent or purge them of potential violence. Perhaps that depends on how scenes of violence are treated and what members of the audience are like; so the audience of an ancient Greek tragedy may have been stimulated in one way and the audience of a contemporary melodrama may be stimulated in another. But the existence and transfer of empathy I take to be a civilizing factor, so long as we can empathize with the victim, not the torturer.

The Roman gladiatorial games probably reinforced bloodthirstiness and a callous disregard for individual life. Then and later, the nobelman had only to repair to his torture chamber after dinner for an evening's entertainment. The Sicilian Bull of Phalaris and the Iron Maiden surely gave delight, but not to their victims or those who could empathize with them. Today's equivalents in enjoyment are regarded as utter depravity, indulged in only by the abnormal. Of course the western world recently witnessed the Nazi concentration camp, which is evidence enough that men are still cruel, but several things should be noted, among them the increasing difficulty of staffing camps, and the apparent need for propaganda to the effect that Jews were in fact not human beings. There was even discussion in a learned German journal about whether, if Jews were mated with apes, they would have offspring. One does not so readily empathize with lower animals, nor do moral rules so easily apply to them.

The drama, which requires empathy, and trains it, has the great virtue of being imaginary; we live in it emotionally and intellectually, but no one is ever really hurt. There is good reason for calling even a tragedy a play because, like play, it is not real as daily life is real: antagonists can shake hands after the event, play hostility forgotten. And the drama is not so simple as sports, nor so rigid in its rules. It is also the most political of the arts. Not only did Plato and Aristotle write about it, but also Rousseau, Hume, and Burke, all political philosophers. For the drama portrays the relations of men to each other as revealed in speech and action, and has regularly included problems of ruling and being ruled.

In all but his most private life, man defines himself, in speech and action, by his relations to other men and to things. The drama shows him as he defines himself, and his world as he understands it. The sociological metaphors of actor and role come from the theater, which is an obvious source of our understanding of human relationships. "All the world's a stage,/And all the men and women merely players" preceded contemporary sociology by some years. But the world stage changes, as it is redefined by the human actors in it. Rome commanded allegiance; Athens did not, at least not in the same way, for the Athenians (not Athens) were themselves the *polis*. And the actors on the theater's stage change, too, as the playwright redefines them. Yet through history actors exist and act in relation to others. The great dramatic conflicts— between Agamemnon and Clytemnestra, Creon and Antigone, Hamlet and Claudius, Faust and Mephistopheles, Hedda and Lövborg—are moral, and whatever its aesthetic problems of form, the content of serious drama is moral conflict.

So the drama portrays constant concern with moral issues, at the same time that it provokes and trains empathy. As tragedy, it also shows what statuses do to the persons who occupy them, and how statuses continue, although persons die. It is tragic that the uniqueness of the person, with his gifts, is gone, and the community suffers from the loss if the gifts were great. But the moral problems remain to confront those who occupy the same statuses in the future. Even when whole nations disappear, as Troy did, their moral problems reappear in the human arrangements of other nations.

In life, as in the drama, some intellectuals internalize the moral conflicts of their time, and can be internally divided by them, Hamlet-like or Faust-like. That internal division is one reason intellectuals, at least intellectuals of this type, make poor rulers. The division may be intensified by empathy: one of two conflicting obligations may be more advantageous to self and the second more advantageous to others, yet the others are sometimes felt as keenly as self, and felt to have more warrant. Empathy, which helps create felt obligation, can thus bring personal crisis when divisions occur. And personal crisis is more widespread when great divisions in the culture are mirrored in the psyche; cultural divisions themselves occurring more frequently in a world of rapid change, in which shared values, ends, and obligations cease to be integrated. The white, Anglo-Saxon Protestant in the United States may feel obligation to his own kind while empathy with blacks may bring conflicting feelings of obligation to their welfare, though it interferes little with his own.

Ours is, in the western world, an age both of complacency and crisis. It is complacent because of its wealth and the opportunities provided by its mobility; it is in crisis because of the pace of change. The intellectual, who feels this division more than others, is himself richer and more secure than in the immediate past, yet hardly able to create categories to contain the last waves of change, or to harden his heart to those who demand still more rapid change because they are not so rich or secure as he. The old categories seem not to apply: the revolutionary young include large groups of the well-to-do, who are not demanding bread and work, but freedom from institutional strictures and power to bring change, which is often unspecified. At the same time the recent dream of "one world" seems naive when the old empires are being replaced by a host of small nations within which every tribe or ethnic group asks for autonomy, and so encourages more fragmentation. It is easy enough to empathize with those who will not trust their cherished ways of life to others (would we?) yet without "one world" we may be committed to endless wars. Every step to meet new demands brings newer demands; neither our national nor our international institutions hold up well in a world in which change has brought a cry for more and speedier change, and there is too little time to weigh the consequences.

In this situation, the intellectual *should* be weighing consequences, exploring alternatives, and making proposals. But for the moment he is paralyzed by the speed of change, internal divisions, and intellectual confusion. Labels of the past do not apply accurately to groups that are not anarchist, syndicalist, or communist, but are indeed revolutionary; and no new labels have yet been invented for them. Intellectuals had barely affixed their last phrases to the phenomena of the time—"the silent generation" to university students, "the end of ideology" to politics—when another generation with an ideology as yet uncharted, screamed dissent. Without a theoretical framework, with few categories of explanation, the intellectual cannot work the separate strands of the time into a pattern. And the pressures to do nothing from the complacent, advancing portion of his culture interfere even with the intellectual preparation and daring needed to provide a new framework and try new categories.

Our increasingly technological economy now needs the intellectual as it once needed labor, and it offers suitable incentives and rewards. But it is not fully as intellectual that the economy needs him, but as technician, to man our burgeoning schools, entertainments, sciences, journals, and advertising. The intellectual in some of his expert functions is omnipresent, in the columns of newspapers, on television, in the classroom, the laboratory, the halls of Congress (because government needs him too), and the offices of business executives. What is required, really, is the intellectual expert, and so the intellectual-as-expert. Advanced technical societies are increasingly complex and increasingly in need of experts of all sorts. In order that experts exist and be available, society trains them in ever-larger numbers. So "intellectual careers" multiply and great centers of learning work at training, refining, and polishing specialists of every kind demanded by the outside society plus, of course, the pedagogue-specialists, who will train the next generation.

Fortunately, the highly trained specialist keeps the social machine functioning and improving at all the things it does. Unfortunately, there are things that need doing that are not done, and there is dissatisfaction in many quarters with what the machine does. The intellectual should be at work on these matters, lest the machine stop. But the intellectual-as-expert is not prepared to deal with such contingencies, nor trained to avoid them. And much of the pool of intellectual ability is drained by the pressure for specialists. In social science and philosophy, the scope of the best minds of the early days of the century seems gone and with it some chances of escaping disaster. Dewey and Russell took strong positions about society and politics. What does Wittgenstein have to say about them? Veblen wrestled with the great problems of human society and has been replaced by excellent technicians.

When the intellectual is divided, he may feel inconsistent obligations with relatively equal strength. When the intellectual-as-expert is deeply committed to his own enterprise, he feels its obligations fully enough for action, but feels contrary obligations little, if at all. Empathy is felt with other experts, and with those who share their values, and genuine hostility is often expressed toward those outside; imagination falters, and sympathy dries up. Such outsiders as rebellious students, angry blacks, and those who feel dispossessed are asked for a bill of particulars, to be stated in acceptable social terms. If grievances cannot be stated and remedies proposed in terms familiar to the experts, it is assumed there are none. Implicit values, ends, and obligations of the dissenters are too rarely explored by the intellectual to discover what they are and to bring the dissenters to greater self-awareness.

Underlying much dissatisfaction and dissent today is, I think, a special form of alienation from the society based on an overwhelming difference between a set of deeply cherished traditional values and social reality. We inherit the democratic, individualistic values of self-government: town-meeting participation in the settlement of our own affairs in our own way and, within social limits, living our personal lives as we please and choosing our careers freely. In the family, the schoolroom, and the pulpit these norms have been iterated and reiterated; they are the value base of our society. Yet in fact so many consequences of our acts are unintended, we live so much in the world of covert function, that society seems scarcely more controlled by man and his values than nature is. This disparity is sensed and felt, rather than perceived, but that is enough to breed an existential despair, and to alienate many of us from the society that permits such disparity.

We made a distinction earlier between what the humanities study: the way men make society; and what the social sciences study: the way society makes man. The plight of modern man results from the imbalance between the two in the lives of most men, in which what they do has little significance for society, while their lives are mostly what is done to them. Of course, even biological nature is full of covert functions, of which "the balance of nature" is a prime example, aided every time an owl kills a field mouse, and people have always been considerably less than all-powerful in society, as in nature. But our situation is not like that of the vast ancient kingdoms of the Near East, in which few had any power, but in which ideologies and norms accorded fairly well with practice. Our society retains the ideologies and norms of smaller, better-integrated communities while it continues to move toward complicated, poorly integrated structures which are nearly incapable of deliberate control. That movement, I think, increases the power of covert functions in our lives, the winds of society and bureaucracy, and decreases the power of decision and overt functions. In the presidential campaign of 1968, most Americans wanted a choice between Rockefeller and McCarthy, but had no chance to make that choice at the polls. This is the kind of thing that is happening more and more frequently.

In smaller, more manageable communities, intended and avowed functions could usually be carried out, and their consequences could be close to what their members wanted. This is still true of small communities today. But we have a sense that such communities are islands which may be flooded at any time by the vast social ocean surrounding them. Increasingly, power is vested in larger or more remote organizations, which are harder to control, and which intervene in, and sometimes destroy, smaller communities. Colleges can be altered suddenly by distant trustees or stafe legislatures, ending at a stroke years of planning and care. Even more meaningless to the participants, a small, thriving farm town can become empty and unpleasant in a few years time, due to the impersonal workings of the economy. What else are infla-tion and depression to most people but social forces that affect them like a sirocco, uncalled for and unmanageable? This is the world of covert function, unrelated to the desire, will, or intel-ligence of the people in it.

Possibly, alienation may decrease a little as we learn about covert functions through social, psychological, and economic laws, and so find a little understanding of our situation. But that knowledge does not help enough because it usually consists of generalizations about what happens to us, not what we make happen. Because we learn the consequences of actions that had other ends, and are on guard for the future, it does not follow that any one, by foregoing such action, could avoid the consequences. If I learn that when money is comparatively plentiful and people spend it freely for goods and services, inflation will result, I cannot prevent that inflation by becoming a miser. The point is that I suffer the results of what other people do, even if no one at all intended those results. As I learn that, I learn how little control I have over my own destiny, and over the social conditions in which I live. And if I have been raised to believe that my society, above all others, allows us to pursue happiness in our own way and manage our own affairs in cooperation with others, it is not surprising if I regurgitate what I have been taught, and feel alienated from the society that teaches it.

The critical, moral program I have been urging can do much more than the standard generalizations about society to let each man feel the meaningfulness of his own actions. The little rule about inflation is valuable for tax laws and the policies of the Federal Reserve Board, and that makes it useful. But it does not place the average citizen in the context of belief and meaning that the problems of critical morality provide. Nor does it relieve, more than slightly, the burden of covert and almost meaningless obligation. To do that requires not just knowledge, but knowledge that can be used by each person to give meaning to his life. That meaningfulness consists fundamentally in three types of action: the application of means to yield ends that realize values; participation in ritual action that creates and enhances community and cohesiveness; aesthetic and intellectual behavior that gives direct satisfaction. When the first of these has to do with shared ends and values, for which the means are social obligations, our actions are especially meaningful because they bring a sense of control, or at least participation, in shaping society.

Meaningfulness in life is eroded by creation of a mass society. For all that has been written on the subject, "mass society" still needs delineation. It is, of course, an approximation of inter-changeable people with interchangeable jobs, a reduction of per-sonality to the identity of replaceable machine parts. Thus it is the opposite of ancient and Renaissance tragedy in which individual death changes everything: with Hector dead, Troy will fall; with Hamlet gone, Norway will rule Denmark. Mass society is born as intermediate organizations are destroyed or lose their significance; that, at least, was the way Durkheim, Tocqueville, and Ortega saw the problem, Durkheim emphasizing work-related organizations. I prefer to put the issue as one of loyalty, an old-fashioned but still workable word. As loyalty to intermediate organizations—unions, churches, political parties, businesses, clubs—is eroded, and only the larger society itself can demand loyalty, some people who were loyal to it when they had other loyalties find they can no longer be loyal to it.

There are many reasons for the inability to be loyal to the larger society alone, but I shall be concerned with one only. Small-er, intermediate organizations are more responsive to individual initiative, and can more readily be directed; the larger society, filled with covert functions, is only in part manageable by those with power and almost unmanageable by the rest. In order to have any effect on the society, most people have to unite, form new groups, and work together. Those groups—organizations to end smog, preserve forests, give more power to students, etc.—are sur-rogates for older intermediate organizations through which the in-dividual had some leverage on society. But where the older organ-izations (churches are a prime example) had continuity and tradi-tional power, the new ones do not, and there is a tendency to create new groups ad hoc to bring about specific rather than con-tinuing ends; this does little to ensure continuity, for when the ends are won—or, sometimes when they are lost—the group is very likely to dissolve. A law to make forests into national parks or an inclusion of students in college governance puts an end to many ad hoc groups.

Powerlessness and meaninglessness may bring alienation as rejection of the larger society and its values, or just its practice. Those so alienated may withdraw from society—in drugs, alcohol, deviance—or participate more fully, often in groups that dissent, demonstrate, or obstruct. The new groups invite loyalty, and may offer solidarity and companionship. They offer temporary release from alienation, but they are transient by nature, and their disappearance only intensifies alienation. Older intermediate groups, too, sometimes provide values which conflict with those of other groups and those of the larger society, but their values are more often supportive. A religion, for example, may breed conscientious objectors in times of war, or revolution in times of tyranny, yet normally support the values of society. When there is a conflict of values, a member of that religion may even prefer the values of the larger society, yet may have been brought to his preference by still other values derived from the religion.

As intermediate groups weaken, the values they provided that supported society weaken with them, and the larger society's values have to stand alone. In addition, the values of society have to be put to the test of a new practice, because formerly they were implemented within intermediate groups. Participation is an obvious example. Local political clubs may elect a talented member to be a city councilman and then to be mayor, senator, and president. Members of the club feel rightly that they had a hand in national destiny, and they may continue to have it, as friends and advisers of a senator or president. If such clubs are wiped out, there is that much less participation and that much more sense of powerlessness in the country.

I do not see the major nations of the west as mass societies, but I think there has been a movement in that direction, from which they all suffer. Intermediate organizations, like class structures, maintain group and individual differences. As those groups weaken, and class structures disappear, we do become more alike and find ourselves more desperately without moorings. Many of us support all moves to bigness and oneness with enthusiasm and with little sense of their consequences apart from the particular ends we have in mind. The ecumenical movement itself, for all its trumpeted virtues, may reduce individual and group differences still further. Yet these differences not only contribute to the variety and spice of life, but allow for cooperation as well as disagreement. Cooperation in a group whose members were totally alike would be limited to the most rudimentary matters, or would be inefficient, for there would be no rational order or stratification, no reason for different members to have different statuses with separate obligations for each status.

One enormous danger in the movement to mass society is possible loss of freedom. Powerful traditions of liberty and deeply felt obligations to permit and support freedom of choice in many areas of life may preserve freedom in mass society, but freedom is often, like religious toleration, a result of the multiplicity and diversity of groups. Too often, freedom exists when a number of competing groups, like religious sects, accept the improbability of any one of them becoming a large majority, and allow all the liberty each asks for itself. Sometimes freedom exists because a man can emasculate opposing group demands and obligations by appealing from one to another and then perhaps back to the first. At one time there was appeal from the Parlement of Paris to the king, to the bishop, and to the pope. Today, too, some such appeals exist: e.g., from an employer to a union, to an arbitration board, and perhaps back to the employer; from one's college chaplain, if one is a Catholic student, to one's parish priest, and then to the bishop.

As other groups lose power, the larger society may gain power, which probably flows to the nation-state, or may become unmanageable because of new and dissident groups that oppose society and each other, or strive competitively for power. The Weimar Republic may have been in the latter situation before the Nazis captured Germany. Under the Third Reich, the government moved deliberately toward a mass society, by stifling family and church, and by substituting organizations sheerly supportive of the state, like the Hitler Jugend, for genuine intermediate groups, like the Boy Scouts.

In mass society, conflict of obligation dwindles. That is not because intermediate organizations actually disappear, although some do, and not because membership in them falls off greatly, although it may, but because loyalty to them fades. Obligations are taken most seriously and usually felt most strongly when members have great loyalty to the groups which demand them. Loyalty is both emotional and intellectual; it is a commitment to someone or something. Perhaps it can be defined in terms of value. Loyalty to a group means a high felt evaluation of the existence and continuance of the group. Ultimate loyalty to a group would be higher evaluation of the existence and continuance of that group than of any other. Loyalty, then, is basic to performance of obligation. Formal membership in any group brings obligations, but they are felt and carried out by virtue of 'loyalty to the group. Although there are exceptions, it is generally the case that the greater the loyalty to a group, the more deeply felt are the obligations demanded by it; and when there is conflict of obligation, the tendency is to accept the obligation of the group that most enlists our loyalty. Conflicts of church and state in different historical periods furnish a wealth of evidence of the shift in obligations fulfilled in more and in less religious ages.

Mass society contains fewer separate loyalities than more traditional society. Alienated men may feel few loyalties of any kind, or some fierce ones; and the nation-state in a mass society may demand, and get, ultimate loyalty. Even when a totalitarian state creates new groups to replace old ones, or retains the name and some of the structure of older groups while changing their content, all groups are subordinate to, or supportive of, the state. Loyalties are quite hierarchical, and all human associations other than the state are in danger of destruction or substantial alteration. Totalitarianism offers an alternative to alienation, though a narrow one: the devout totalitarian is not alienated, although others in the same society may be. Supportive groups may even evoke loyalties from those who would not feel great loyalty to the nation-state alone. Such people, if they never give the state ultimate loyalty, may discover conflicts of obligation, however well-integrated the groups are. A neighborhood organization, for example, which centers on playing chess, watching your neighbors, and occasionally discussing official theory may help create chess players and close friends, two groups which can develop obligations antithetical to those owed the state.

Erosion of loyalty to a democratic government, a phenomenon bred by the general dissolution of loyalties in any movement toward a mass society, replaces opposition with dissent. By opposition I mean something akin to a political party in loyal opposition, when what it opposes is not democratic government, but another political party in power at the time. There is no diminution of loyalty in the opposition, just objection to governmental policies, and a bid for its own power within the system. "Dissent" I shall use as the opposite of "consent"; it is a withdrawal of loyalty from one's own group or system. A concomitant of that withdrawal is a rejection of the obligations of members. Typically, those who dissent from their government accept no obligation to fight for it; those who oppose policies or parties still consent to the government, and accept the same obligations as those they oppose (sometimes with the exception of conscientious objection to a particular policy).

Opposition and dissent have different areas of choice. Since opposition is within a group and includes loyalty to it, the choices of those in opposition are in some cases the choices of any member of the group, but in other cases are choices among ways of altering group policy or removing from power those who made that policy. The great limitation on those in opposition is that they must reject any choice that ensures the overthrow of policy or their own acquisition of power if it also alters the nature or basic structure. of the group. No opposition political party, for example, may take power if it must then suppress future elections. But when the desire for power or the feeling of obligation to enact new policy are stronger than the value set on group survival or political process, opposition becomes dissent. Dissent is also bred by the conviction that the group's structure—not just those temporarily in political office—will not permit a change of power relations in it or an alteration in policy, and that only change in the nature of the group can bring those things about. The greatest danger to one who dissents from a group and devotes his energies to that *alone*, is that he will succeed. For groups are not followed by vacuums but by other groups, and success in dissent should be coupled with success in construction. Revolutionists whose whole life is revolution are usually worthless in post-revolutionary societies for which they are not prepared.

Society, groups within it, and the nation-state share a common weakness. Loyalty to them is often less than loyalty to classes, or statuses, within them. There is not only Aristotle's war between the rich and the poor in society and the nation-state, but enmity, or at least ill-will, between farmers and industrial workers, businessmen and academicians, even the new and the old aristocracy of wealth or title. Marx foresaw a division of nations along economic class lines, so that French and German workers or French and German businessmen would feel more in common with each other than with their own compatriots. That is indeed often the case, but the varied forces of nationalism have so far prevented international class war. Yet loyalty to an economic class is only one of what may be called the status-loyalties of society.

In any large group, and even in some small ones, a loyalty is bred to a subgroup composed of similar statuses, or of statuses with some equivalence in rank. Too often for the stability of the group, such loyalty is invidious: status-loyalty finds its interests satisfied at the expense of those in other statuses. When this goes far, it is a cause of group disorganization. The whole moral fabric of the group rots, because statuses within the group have different obligations which, woven together, once made the fabric. The shared ends of the group are best attained when the obligations falling on each status are so coordinated that the group as a whole carries out means that yield its ends. When they are invidious, status-loyalties clash with group loyalties, obligations conflict, and new status obligations (those of a subgroup) are generated. The new obligations may enjoin acting in such a way as to repel advantages of another subgroup, which are regarded as incursions. So a manufacturer may feel he is disloyal to his peers if he grants certain union demands, although they are demands of his own workers, and may be troubled by his conscience for doing so, even if granting the demands is good for his business and the economy. The same situation exists when white Protestant union members find other ethnic and religious groups entering the labor market and seeking union membership, and when white union members find black applicants.

Since status-loyalty may be stronger than group loyalty, subgroup obligations may be felt more intensely than group obligations. The Cagoulards rejected the Popular Front in France, saying "Rather Hitler than Blum," and the first article in the constitution of some American radical parties was "Defense of the Soviet Union." The strength of a subgroup is usually less than that of its group, and it may therefore seek alliance with a rival group which seems to have ends and obligations that favor the subgroup. In such cases, a simple rationality would dictate that members of the subgroup resign from their original group and join that of the rival, but love of custom and desire for victory are not easily eradicated. Subgroup members are more likely to become quasi-traitors than to change their memberships. The custom-loving man hates to give up one way of life for another, and the intellectual hates to give up a chance to bring about the program he supports; both are likely to stay home while they praise and work with (or for) the rival group, rather than join it. The confusion in obligation that results can bring about all manner of shifts in loyalty, and by remaining in the group from which they dissent, members keep alive the option of reviving their loyalty to it. The enormous turnover in membership in the American Communist Party shows how many are moved to a dissent which is followed by the consent that once preceded it.

Rarely does enough thought go into these shifts in loyalty and obligation; they are usually a step-by-step process until the thing is accomplished, rather than a crisis of conscience resolved by deliberate decision. Part of the fault lies in a society that demands many loyalties but has little serious concern with thought and discussion of the obligations that go with loyalties, the academy being as remiss in this as the rest of society. Part lies in the moral complexity of modern life, in which the growth in obligation and choice has not been matched by the necessary growth in moral thought. To be serious and useful, moral thought must be combined with social, psychological, and political thought, and must use the categories of several disciplines to deal with actual moral problems as they appear in human life. We begin to see this as we talk about pollution of the environment and increase in population, two related problems. We cannot come to solutions based on the categories of chemistry and religion alone, but need many others as well, from politics, psychology, ecology, business, and so on. Yet without basic moral decision all our other knowledge is useless, because we do not know what we ought to do.

Instead of growing, moral thought has shrunk, for attempts of all sorts have been made to deal with moral matters in non-moral terms. Frequently psychological health and illness have substituted for good and evil, perhaps as a result of psychoanalysis, and in the process, social obligation has disappeared. But other choices have been made, as well as health and illness, to replace obligation. Sometimes value or norm preempts the entire field of ethics, especially among sociologists, and sometimes responses and conditioning replace ethics altogether, especially for psychologists. The dire necessity of obligation, without which society cannot function, is often disregarded by those just mentioned and by economists, businessmen, and technicians as well. Moral problems mount, but moral thought is replaced by other modes of thought which use other categories. It is not just scientists who thus denigrate the moral life but the bourgeoisie and, following them, many others. The scientist and the bourgeois seem to offer very different reasons for minimizing morality, but I suspect there is a connection and I should like to suggest what it is.

Freedom does not exist without choice, and freedom grows as choice grows. When men are offered no more than the necessities of life, little choice exists, but a wealth of possibilities increases choice. It seemed necessary in the late Roman Empire to fix men through life in the jobs, statuses, and prestige of their fathers; it seems desirable, today, to have as much mobility as possible. In addition, technology adds choice and the problems of choice in bewildering variety. The difference in the amount of choice between Roman and American must be enormous. We should be able to conclude that as choice of all kinds grows, moral choice grows too. Why would we not find moral problems everywhere in the choices we meet, and be face to face with unthought-of dilemmas as each day offers new possibilities? And surely most of the old moral difficulties remain while new ones burgeon? Perhaps just because that is so, because moral choices are often so painful to make and because the new moral problems are indeed bewildering, almost defying solution, we are happy to deny moral quality to all choices whatever. After all, it is much simpler and enormously less painful to choose on the basis of, say, efficiency and desire than on the basis of obligation and value.

Yet escape as we may, the moral quality is even more characteristic of man—of the very meaning of man—than the rational quality which Aristotle chose, and man is better defined as moral than as rational: lesser breeds have some reason but no morality, and the traditional God is conceived as rational, but also perfectly good, and so is really beyond morality in the human sense. Human morality requires a being capable of evil as well as good, a being, therefore, for whom choice can be moral, not just efficient. Although so much of the new erosion of morality comes from scientific romanticism, its results suit and support a society which can claim that science justifies its moral attitudes. It is a society whose moral problems are enormous and whose large middle class is willing to deal with those problems in familiar coin—the terms of business, science, expertise, energy, profit-and-loss, power—but not in the painful, soul-searching language of morality, which could keep it from—perhaps bring it to reject—the "good life" it has provided for itself, which usually means no more than abundance and leisure.

That "good life" itself needs evaluation which it is not receiving, for the evaluation must be moral—it cannot be anything else and be important—yet the very possibility of intelligent moral appraisal, which would include the suggestion and dissection of alternatives, is now being denied. For hundreds of years men have been guided by the vision of a rich society, abundant in opportunity, leisure, and education. It was a moral vision, dictated by the belief that such a society was the necessary condition, or the means, for most men to be able to pursue their happiness effectively, and, in short, to lead the good life. Generations of men have struggled to make the vision a reality and, at last, have succeeded magnificently, despite areas of dark neglect. At this moment we have what we wanted, but now that we see what it is, many of us don't like it. The reason, I suspect, is that we wanted the wrong things, or the right things in the wrong way; we concentrated so long on material conditions we thought necessary to the good life and devoted so little thought to the good life itself—to the intelligent uses of wealth, leisure, and education—that we have converted the means into the end. And as an end, the abundant society is not enough.

So we have entered a new world—whose model, for good or evil, is America—ill-equipped to deal with the overwhelming problem of how to live well in it. Many of us respond to the problem by talking of taste, inclination, and freedom: let every man do with the new situation as he likes. Others, in astonishing numbers, refuse to put up with the new society at all. Traditional religion and morality no longer hold them, and development of a new morality is beyond most people's powers.

Opposition to the social order has been common enough through all history. When responsible, it is usually accompanied by a list of grievances and a series of proposed remedies, the grievances almost always real and the remedies sometimes correct. The most distressing aspect of the opposition today is that whatever the grievances specified and the reforms justified, the underlying grievance, the base of the disorder, is everywhere the same: life has been emptied of moral significance. To get richer and live better when one is already fairly rich and lives quite well, as the middle class does, is hardly a bugle call to stir the blood, nor has it any moral quality. To aid the genuinely deprived and the relatively deprived, to end hunger and provide opportunity, are causes to enlist in, causes worthy of moral fervor. But the sad fact remains that these are old causes, for which men fought and bled for centuries. They are causes in which we have had notable, if imperfect, success. The causes are completely worthy, but they are not enough to banish the void, because when they, too, are won, we are going to be confronted again with emptiness.

Those who scent the emptiness, mostly among the young, have moved from opposition to dissent. There is a frightening quality of nihilism about some of them, young Nechayevs who find their societies moribund but not ready to die for a long time, and who decide to give the *coup de grâce*. It is as though, like Nechayev, they carried in secret cipher *The Catechism of the Revolutionist* which says of the revolutionist, "He knows only one science, the science of destruction . . . . The object is but one—the quickest possible destruction of that ignoble system." If their object is indeed but one, they have no concern with what comes after destruction. Please do not accuse me of capriciousness in mentioning *The Catechism*. It is being sold at the moment of this writing by at least one young group, not in cipher but in plain English.

Many of those who have chosen dissent are not unlike people in opposition. They are interested in new life-styles, like group marriages in Sweden, group unmarriages in the United States, work if possible outside or on the fringes of ordinary business, experimentation with drugs, sexual promiscuity, and sometimes crime. Most experiments are failures; Ehrlich discovered Salvarsan after 605 failures; and most or all of these experiments will be failures, too, at least as guides for a whole society. But what is revealed is, I think, clear. A great many young people and some of their elders refuse to put up with what they often call sham and hypocrisy, with a society that denies its moral base and has nothing to take its place but at best convention and at worst cupidity and ruthlessness. Indeed another complaint of the young, the apathy of so many in the face of distress and danger, is explicable as the apathy of those without moral conviction.

There is probably no return to the old certitudes. But we have replaced them with nothing equally moral in tone, only with that "good life" which is hollow. Not to overstate the case wildly, I admit at once that there are moral men, even moral and angry social scientists who are unaware of the aid they offer by their determinist or behaviorist convictions to the men they are angry at. There are committed artists and scientists, judges, teachers, and surgeons, by the thousands. What I have been describing is something else: the general quality of life created in rich societies by a failure of morality and a lack of significance, even—I hope it does not sound too petty—by a colossal failure of taste. The enormous problems of international politics, destruction of the natural environment, overpopulation, and the mechanization of life do not engage us as a society, do not absorb our energies, give us no goals. We evade them all and continue in a lethargy of drift. If we were to sound the charge and attack in full force most of our problems of alienation and anger would vanish. Even the genuine and trained intellectuals in our nations have, in the great majority, foregone their functions by not inquiring into our ills and proposing remedies.

Of course, one difficulty in saying anything critical and intelligent about our world is that it was not imposed on us by others; it is not a result of tyranny or ruthlessness; it is ours because we made it, and we made it because we wanted to. In other situations we might still want this world of ours: to a hungry man a full belly seems happiness enough. But to the well-fed man who no longer struggles for survival, there is a real question of what he should strive for, since strive he must; it is the human condition. Preeminence, riches, power—except for the few who use them like drugs—are dust and ashes when we get them, and all wisdom has said so. Of course, there is an answer, and one not difficult to find. It is not the hopelessness of a disorder with no solution that bothers us, but our total unreadiness to state the answer and act on it.

We are very much like the man who wants—he says— to write, but needs time and money to do so. When, finally, a beneficent foundation or institution, or his own enterprise, gives him money enough to buy time, and he stares at the white paper before him, he may find that although he has none of his usual excuses for not writing, he had better find others quickly, because he cannot bring himself to smudge the virgin page with an inky word. We, too, as a civilization, find excuses for refusing to see an answer to a question we do not ask, and so have no difficulty whatever in not acting on it.

Our best excuse for doing nothing is the reduction of morality to what we are trained to do: deal with our countless problems in terms of business, science, technology, or expertise. But the way to answer our great question about how to live in the society of abundance and leisure is, of course, first to treat that society as a means not an end: to use our leisure to consider the moral problems of our time, all the problems I have mentioned, and many more, and to fashion an idea of the good life in moral terms; then to use our riches so that as many people as possible can do the same, *and act on our conclusions.* Since what we have, technically and materially, is wonderful, something men never had before, new possibilities are open. The question of whether it benefits mankind ultimately to have wealth and leisure—so few people throughout the world do; so many can—may remain speculative. It is like asking whether an imperialist nation should have a colony, when it has already had it for a long time. Perhaps it should not have had it—in what terms do we make that judgment? moral ones—but that does not mean it should flee at once, abandoning people who may not be ready to rule themselves, even though perhaps they once did. The issue is, granting the fact of colonization, what is the best thing to do *now*?

We can conquer hunger, we can give leisure, we can use the machine to eliminate serfdom. But we must be wary that wealth and leisure do not corrupt, as they may so easily. Here our need is for a full acceptance of man's moral nature, which includes his great capacity for evil, and the moral nature of so many of the problems we face. Emphatically, we must not merely devise social means that yield already postulated ends; we must reevaluate and then alter the ends we have inherited. That new evaluation will require all we know and all the categories relevant to man and society, bringing us a new social science and a new philosophy. The contemporary world contains unparalleled problems—it should be obvious we approach Armageddon—but unparalleled opportunities. It is time to condemn our excuses and begin an examination of ourselves and our new world in scientific, humanistic, and, above all, moral terms. For soon, very soon, we must act.